DATE DUE

MAR 1 1993			

Warsaw Visitor

Tales from the Vienna Streets

The last two plays
of
WILLIAM SAROYAN

Edited and with an Introduction by
Dickran Kouymjian

The Press
at
California State University, Fresno
Fresno, CA 93740

Warsaw Visitor and *Tales from the Vienna Streets*
Copyright © 1991

Printed in the United States of America

Copy editing by Carla Jean Millar
Production supervised by Rosie Gutierrez
Cover design by George McCann

Orders should be addressed:

The Press at California State University, Fresno
Fresno, CA 93740

To Angèle

with love

CONTENTS

PREFACE

During the four years since *An Armenian Trilogy,* the first volume in this series of unpublished plays by William Saroyan, was released, Saroyan's plays, both early and late, have continued to be performed regularly throughout the world. There have been several new collections of his prose works, and a number of studies about him have been published. Also a major biography is in preparation under the auspices of the William Saroyan Foundation. The plays in this volume further attest to both the quantity and quality of literature left unpublished when Saroyan died.

Warsaw Visitor and *Tales from the Vienna Streets* were plays Saroyan wrote during his last summer in Paris. Barring the unexpected, they may be considered his ultimate theatrical statements. Although different in style, theme, and length they have a special kinship, belonging as they do to Saroyan's own experiences during that final year. He had been in Warsaw in May and Vienna in June. The stages of those journeys and the nature of his reflections were no doubt recorded in his carefully kept journals, but that was often not enough for Saroyan. He liked to transform into play form, or perhaps, better, dramatic dialogue, what he had lived through, thus adding overtones of meaning to the raw materials of experience. These plays, however, are in no sense autobiography in conversational form; they are vital theatrical pieces written to be performed.

Among their many riches, both plays include controversial themes: homosexuality in *Tales from the Vienna Streets,* and death—his own, by cancer—in *Warsaw Visitor.* Saroyan had already treated terminal cancer as a subject in an earlier play, *Don't Go Away Mad* (1947, published 1949), which was shunned by Broadway producers, shocked that such a subject be proposed for popular New York theater even though the writer was famous. Clearly Saroyan's theater was never conventional nor conformist. And the price he paid for that militant iconoclasm was the disfavor of most establishment critics, with whom he battled verbally in the introductions and postscripts he added to the published versions of his plays. Saroyan always felt those critics were too rigidly bound by the customary canons of playwriting to be able to understand properly, let alone appreciate, his unorthodox theater.

William Saroyan was never to see another summer after the one in which he wrote these plays. He was never to travel again to Paris, let alone Warsaw and Vienna, as he had from May through August of 1980. It was the end of his journey, and these plays are the closing chapters of his creativity. They are among his last words, and as he said mockingly in each of them, "famous last words," the dying playwright's own. This lends a special attraction to what this most prolific and successful American playwright has to tell us, knowing that he will never have a chance to do so again.

Besides theme, both plays are also intriguing because of their unique construction. In *Warsaw Visitor* Saroyan appears both as a character, a writer visiting Poland, and also as Saroyan, the author of the play, standing on the stage describing the behavior of Saroyan the traveler on that same stage. *Tales from the Vienna Streets,* with its song and dance routines, also marks a different format from Saroyan's usual one. It is as if, knowing that the end is near, he is seeking out a new beginning.

*   *   *

In preparing these works for publication I have supplied the cast of characters, the setting, and the time of the action for *Warsaw*

Visitor, since they were lacking in the manuscript, and I have divided the play into two acts of five and seven scenes respectively as seemed natural from the context. Needless to say I have scrupulously left the texts exactly as Saroyan wrote and edited them.

Once again I would like to thank the William Saroyan Foundation and its President, Robert Setrakian, for agreeing to the continuation of this William Saroyan Theater series, which keeps intact the strong ties between the author and California State University, Fresno.

For important information crucial to a better understanding of the plays I am obliged to Dr. Franz Schafranek, Director of Vienna's English Theatre, Vienna, Austria, and Dr. Artin Jibilian, Saroyan's physician in Fresno, California. I also thank Gail Sarkisian of Fresno and Ben Amirkhanian, Chairman of Fresno's annual William Saroyan Festival, for sharing with me details about Saroyan pertinent to this volume. Once again Carla Millar, Managing Editor of The Press at CSUF, and Rosie Gutierrez, Production Director, deserve thanks for their care with the technical aspects of the books. Professor Jacqueline Doyle, Senior Editor, reviewed my editing of the plays carefully and patiently prepared with me their presentation. Finally, I would like to thank Dr. Joseph Satin, Director of The Press, not only for his encouragement, but for his commitment to Saroyan's theater, and especially for sharing with me his thoughts on the ultimate meaning of these last plays.

Dickran Kouymjian
Paris, September 24, 1990

INTRODUCTION

William Saroyan wrote *Warsaw Visitor* and *Tales from the Vienna Streets* in Paris during June and July of 1980. He had cancer and knew it. He died less than a year later on May 18, 1981 in the Veteran's Hospital in Fresno, the city where he was born on August 31, 1908. Were these then his last plays? I am not sure and have not wanted to investigate too far in order to allow for the surprises always associated with Saroyan. He was an interior man gifted with a dramatic public presence. He did not talk with others about his writing projects. My files record no later works written in Paris before his departure in late August, and no play titles after *Tales from the Vienna Streets.* When we spoke and met in Fresno in September 1980 and after, he always said he was writing. In November he showed me a thick pile of typed sheets which he said was his journal for the month of October. In a letter sent to me in Paris in March 1981, he repeated that he was writing regularly.

For the moment, then, these can be considered his last plays and among his final works. Today, everyone knows what a prolific writer Saroyan was. He left hundreds of unpublished works in every medium and thousands of fascinating letters. This second volume in the Fresno series of his unpublished plays unites two works devoted to themes emblematic of Saroyan's theater from the beginning. The one written first, *Warsaw Visitor,* deals with death, Saroyan's own, but is anchored firmly in the continuity of living. *Tales from the Vienna Streets* portrays the hilarious and ridiculous world of mortals through the bathos of universally archetypal characters thrown together in a public environment—a cafe—in the international and neutral city of Vienna.

These are not the only themes treated in the plays, nor are they to be regarded as the poles of Saroyan's writing. Yet, life and death and their meaning were to occupy the most important place in the writer's reflections on existence in his final years. One need only remember the titles of his last two published memoirs, *Obituaries* and *Births,* the latter published posthumously, but written between June 23 and July 22, 1979, the former published earlier in 1979, but written during the early months of 1977. Already in 1963 he had published a fascinating memoir entitled *Not Dying,* and in the winter and spring of 1980, while in Fresno, he turned out a long manuscript entitled ''More Obituaries.''

Obituaries has been acclaimed by reviewers as a daring and highly creative autobiological reminiscence, despite its curious inception and structure. It is a long book based on the names of those theater personalities who died in 1976 as published in the January 1977 issue of *Variety.* Saroyan discusses those he knew and didn't know, but reflects throughout on the human condition, saying exactly what he feels about death without fear of reprobation for his frank pronouncements on matters usually avoided. The structure of the book, rather its lack of editing, was disparaged by several commentators, because Saroyan wrote it off the top of his head, refusing to check dates, names, or facts. He contractually prevented the editors at Creative Arts Books in Berkeley from making any editorial corrections or changes. There are 135 sections, each a single paragraph several pages long, full of those wonderful page-long sentences that Saroyan so perfectly and instantly crafted.

If there were any readers of Saroyan who still believed the assertions of certain establishment critics of the forties and fifties that he was a writer of light and sentimental tales designed to provide escape from the brutal realities of his time, *Obituaries* should have forced them to reassess that cliche. As I have remarked in the introduction to *An Armenian Trilogy,* Saroyan was a philosopher with a strong attraction to existentialism. His attitude toward being and ceasing to be was always complex and poly-dimensional. During his final summer he chose in *Warsaw Visitor* to chronicle an illness against which he was struggling without medical aid and without much expectation of survival. He did not brood; he had no time to be gloomy or just wait to see what would happen. A month after he finished *Warsaw Visitor,* in that same summer of 1980, he took up the challenge of a commission to sing the glorious and absurd nature of living in the multi-cultural environment of Vienna through the second play in this volume.

Warsaw Visitor: **The Circumstances of Creation**

Saroyan was much admired in Eastern Europe. During the last four years of his life he visited its various parts four times. His works were very popular, translated and retranslated regularly in Russian, Polish, Czech, Hungarian, Bulgarian, Serbian, Slovak, and Croatian, usually in large editions. He never hid his dislike for the Communist governments of these countries, while affirming his fondness for their people and traditions. His insistence that the people would soon change these regimes was prophetic. He was invited along with other American writers by the U.S.I.A. to make a five nation—Poland, Czechoslovakia, Hungary, Romania, Bulgaria—tour of the area in the late spring of 1980. He accepted against his doctor's wishes, but only after he had finished "a big book in Fresno." He whimsically alludes to it in Scene 5, Act Two of *Warsaw Visitor:* "When the Government itself. . .invited me to visit Warsaw, I replied, Boys and girls, let me just finish this book I am writing, perhaps the most important of my whole career, 'Adios Muchachos,'. . . and I shall be glad to consider accepting your kind invitation. So I am here, for I did indeed finish the great book."

In a memorandum of December 1985, Robert Setrakian, President of the William Saroyan Foundation, asked if I had any information about a work he was informed of by the author's nephew Hank Saroyan, his brother Henry's son. Saroyan told Hank about the "existence of a full length novel. . .entitled *'Adios Amigos'* (or something very similar). Mr. Saroyan advised his

3

nephew of its completion and that it was his desire to have it edited by a literary editor for publication.'' Thus far I have heard nothing further about it, but it is the opus whose completion freed Saroyan to travel to Poland.

Since the late 1950s he spent much of each year in Europe. In 1960 he bought a flat in Paris. This afforded him the freedom of coming and going whenever he wanted, and created a permanent link with Europe. Having already given up living on the beach in Malibu in 1958, he returned to Fresno permanently in 1969 where he bought a house, then two, in a new but modest development to the northwest of where he grew up. During his last twenty years he did his writing and living in Fresno and Paris. From there he traveled freely and regularly, restlessly experiencing and seeing as much as he could. He seemed to be at home everywhere, but as he made clear in his play *Bitlis,* nowhere, in fact, was home.

Observing and recording were fundamental to Saroyan's creative process. Wherever he went he took short notes; whomever he met he questioned, at times endlessly, about the details of his or her life. Scraps of paper were quickly filled with names, dates, miscellany. Titles of plays and stories, novels and essays were jotted down incessantly; most of them got written. Usually it was a title that started a new work, and in these latter years nearly every day was a working day for Saroyan and nearly each of these days produced a new work or a chapter of one. Though I have written about Saroyan's writing habits more than once, it seems important each time a new work is published to describe once again just how he created. There were no outlines or synopses, always a single typed draft, which was edited with pen if it was later sent for publication or production. But since the major portion of the writing of his late years was never sent to publishers, it is preserved exactly as it was first typed.

Works varied in size: short, 1,000-2,000 words; medium, 5,000-10,000 words; long, over 20,000 words. Whatever the subject or literary form, all were written at nearly the same pace: between 2,000 and 2,500 words an hour, usually in half-hour sessions on consecutive days until finished. Not uncommonly, several works were written at the same time, that is, serially on the same days. All of this in addition to his journals and correspondence, which were regular and voluminous. Saroyan was a workaholic. When he was not standing at the typewriter composing, he was accumulating through observation the raw material for the same or the next day's writing. The two plays in this volume were written following this formula.

Warsaw Visitor: The Play

One of the major stops of the five country tour was Warsaw. Saroyan was there at least ten days from May 16 to 26, probably arriving a few days earlier. His journal for the month of May is divided into two parts, from the first to the 12th and from the 12th on into summer, suggesting he might have left the U.S. for Poland on or near that date. After the tour he arrived "home" in Paris on Saturday, June 14 from Belgrade, Yugoslavia. Two days later at 11:40 AM he began *Warsaw Visitor,* which he intended, according to the header on page one, to be a "7-day Play Monday through Sunday June 16 to 22nd," adding at the top of the first page, "Make it Great." But uncharacteristically he continued writing an extra five days. There was no title at first, just two quotations as substitute: "I Have Seen the Future, and It Works, Lincoln Steffens 1929," "I Have Seen Everything. And Nothing Works, William Saroyan 1980." By the second day the title became "Nothing Works." On June 20th it became "California Traveler" in the morning but "Armenian Traveler" in the afternoon session. Three days later the final title, "Warsaw Visitor," was settled on. As he got into the play he seemed to be driven by it. The first day involved only a single warm-up session of half an hour, producing the usual one long closely typed 800 word page. On the second day there were morning and afternoon sessions of forty minutes each, then three sessions a day for ten days, except for one more two-session day (the fourth) and a four-session day, four pages (the sixth day). On the last six days he worked continuously for an hour and twenty minutes. In all he typed thirty-three pages, 27,000 words, in fifteen and a half hours.

Insistence on these details will probably seem tedious to some. But is it not important in such a personal play as this one to know the circumstances of composition? To know that Saroyan poured it out as quickly as he could type? And that its raw state, this first version, would have been little modified—a few words added, a few dropped—had he prepared the script for production? Of course it is important, and we as readers want to know as much as possible. Like Hemingway, Saroyan was obsessed by his craft and very careful about detail. Saroyan could relate immediately what he experienced with style and form. He had the traditional knack of a storyteller, a poet a step away from the living oral tradition of the Near East. As in almost all of his work, he speaks to the reader directly, candidly, with a freshness and honesty that is disarming. If there are contradictions, so what; life is built on paradox and confusion. Some day the actual chronology of the trip can be easily reconstructed from Saroyan's detailed and typed journals which he maintained until he entered the hospital for the last time.

As was common in the later typescripts of his plays, Saroyan made no indication of the division of the work into acts or scenes and left virtually no stage directions. He would provide this information only when it was accepted for publication or if it had been commissioned for performance. More often than not, each working session of one page represented a scene and was so labeled at the top of the page. Thus the number of pages equaled the number of scenes, an arbitrary way of sectioning that seldom corresponded to the natural transitions in the work.

I believe the first page of the typescript was intended as a Prologue, following the usage of the *Book of Job* and Goethe's *Faust,* because Saroyan sets the stage here for the events to follow. I have divided the rest of the play into two acts with five and seven scenes. In the Prologue, Saroyan as Moustache, the writer, tells us plainly his life's plan, starting with his youthful decision to choose art as a way of living, quickly discovering that art and life are the same. From the beginning Saroyan's working method has been unvaried. He has described it numerous times, but perhaps never so succinctly as in this opening: ''I went everywhere and saw everybody and everything and came home to myself and this infernal machine. . . . and put down in simple words what I had seen and heard.'' He worked feverishly, perhaps even in a second state. One thinks of Franz Kafka who, like Saroyan, wrote his novel *The Castle* in a single sitting, trance-like, and made no changes after. In Saroyan's final article for Paris's *International Herald Tribune* entitled ''Tension and Writing and Obits in Variety,'' published on August 27, 1980, he elaborates on his ecstasy while writing:

> It has been my experience from the very beginning of writing, and I mean from the first days of putting words slowly and neatly on lined paper at school, that there is tension in writing. . . . And then when I went into the thing with everything I had, the tension increased so much it seemed to efface time, place, and person, myself; the thing to be made, by writing, became pretty much the only thing, the thing lost inside the unknown of the beginning of things, of systems, the universe. . . in a straight line forever everywhere, and straight into you, and after your flash of being, straight out of you, leaving you a name in Variety. Reader, sometimes long before I was 20 years old, after I had worked for as little as three hours on a work of art in the form of writing, . . . as little as half an hour, obliterating self, time, and place, and I came to, came out of it, what do you think I saw in my own face as I stood and pissed and glanced in the bathroom mirror? I saw somebody else, myself but somebody else, not myself alone, as it had been when I hadn't concentrated on the production of art with so much intensity. It was all of my people, all unknown to me, it was the human race itself.

Autobiography and Theater

From the beginning of his career, Saroyan almost always wrote directly out of his own experience. In his last years he was devoted to an exploration of the self. *Warsaw Visitor* is a minute examination of how a writer, while dying, continues to live as he had always done. The three major characters of the play—the Devil, Moustache and Saroyan—represent different aspects of

Saroyan's own reality. Moustache is the American-Armenian writer traveling to Warsaw for the U.S.I.A., interacting with officials, other writers, and the Poles. The Devil is supposed to represent the dark side of his personality, but is almost likeable and certainly not satanic. In the play he speaks only with Moustache, who recognizes him as his alter-ego: "You are myself, and if I am not thyself,...it comes to the same thing (Act One, Scene 5)." The Devil is also used to point out all of Saroyan's defects, the ones he was most accused of: ill-mannered, over-talkative, demanding center stage and all the attention, childish and foolish. Finally, there is Saroyan the writer in Paris, typing the play about his own visit a month earlier, offering occasional comments, explanations, and analyses to the audience about his characters and the meaning of their actions.

There is no wager made, at least not openly, between Moustache and the Devil, except that at the end of the Prologue, the travel-weary writer, to get rid of his over-talkative counterpart, says, "Just let me sleep.... Is it a deal, Sir?" To which the Devil replies: "You know perfectly well the only deal I make, for it is in all of the legends, poems, stories, plays, operas, and ballets of life." Saroyan refers quite openly to Goethe and to the Faust legend, with its noble and ancient theme and its implications of the writer-intellectual's confrontation with living and dying. On the other hand there is some confusion about the opera, for Moustache talks about Mozart, who did not choose it for a subject, and ignores Gounod, whose Faust is the most popular. I have suggested elsewhere that *Haratch,* the play he wrote a year earlier in the summer of 1979, like *Warsaw Visitor,* consciously chose the form and theme of another classic, Plato's *Symposium.*

The Themes

The major theme of the play is death, yet the play is neither tragic nor morbid. There are several minor themes: the bankruptcy of the Communist system, and its cruel aggression against personal creation, about which Saroyan is uncompromising. This position was a bold one for a writer so loved, praised and solicited in Eastern Europe and the Soviet Union, especially ten years ago, before anyone ever heard of Gorby or *perestroika*. But his satire is not only directed against openly totalitarian regimes. There is also much ridicule of his fellow American writers on the trip and the officials who run various U.S. agencies abroad. As usual Saroyan is a merciless social critic who gets in his digs against organized institutions including his own government. He was always thoroughly anti-establishment. That the world is hardly a just or benevolent place is self evident for him, but the responsibility for this state of affairs rests squarely on everyone; each individual is guilty of the collective crimes of humanity. Early in the play in a long dream sequence he also directs his anger toward wife and children.

Another motif is the constant interference of one's past with the present. This is part of his persistent exercise of remembering in order to understand how what is came to be.

Saroyan and the Jews

A final important theme in the play is the fate of the Jews. Individual scenes are devoted to visits to the Jewish Theatre of Warsaw, the Jewish Cemetery and the Jewish Museum of the city. Saroyan's eloquent defense of recent Jewish history and his devotion to the courageous survival of the Jews should bury forever the baseless and injurious accusations made against him in the biographies by his son Aram, *William Saroyan* (1983) and Lawrence Lee and Barry Gifford, *Saroyan, A Biography* (1984). Collectively, the long sections on the Jews of Poland and the value to humankind of the diaspora rank among the most compassionate and sensitive on the subject in modern literature. As an Armenian who strongly identified with the suffering of his own people, Saroyan underlines the natural empathy he feels for the Jews. This attitude serves as the major thrust for such a statement as, "the Jewish people are the people who have always been nearest to the human soul," uttered during the visit to the Jewish Museum in Act Two, Scene 6. Or further in the same sequence commenting on Auschwitz and Buchenwald: ". . . the Jewish dead are different from all of the other dead murdered by the rest of us—oh yes, we did it, . . . it was not just the Germans, it was not just Hitler and his big fat skinny sick brilliant stupid clever dirty partners who always always only followed orders, as they kept saying at the Nuremberg trials—it was us, old boy, us, us, and I mean us.''

Sickness and Death

The dead and death are central to this play, which Saroyan himself calls a dramatic memoir. When the Devil in Act Two, Scene 5 asks him if he is ''thinking Death,'' Moustache replies, ''Yes, I am thinking Death, but I have always thought of Death. How could I possibly not have done so? It is there at the center of us.'' Moustache is dying, physically; the Devil says it first early in the play: ''He's dying, he knows it, he doesn't believe it (Act One, Scene 3).'' Then in the same scene the writer repeats it to the Devil-turned-doctor, whose prognostication was cancer of the prostate. ''I don't like the diagnosis which already is established...and has already killed me.... Doc, my reply is this: in your language, yes, I have cancer, in my language, it is myself that I have, another variation of myself.'' ''Never mind the cancer part,'' he says in Act Two, Scene 3, ''everybody has got to have something and there is cancer in the Saroyan family.... A tribe will have cancer in its chemistry for centuries and it will do the job of allowing passage out.'' By such language Saroyan shows us how he has come to terms with his imminent end, not hesitating to describe from time to time the sensation of the cancer's growth and the resultant discomfort. But Saroyan's grace saves us as witnesses to his dying, as his acceptance of the illness and its integration into his personal history saves him. There is neither life nor death for Saroyan, only various forms of being.

In a remarkable speech in the penultimate scene of *Warsaw Visitor* Saroyan describes his actual existence at the moment of writing:

> ...death has come to me. Oh, I'm still alive and still kicking, which means I am still fighting out each day's demands on me to survive and to make the most of every moment in Budapest, then in Bucharest, then in Belgrade, and finally back in my own flat in Paris...in all of those places and among all of the activities in which I figured I was dying,

I was indeed dead or as good as dead but still wandering around, and this is the part that keeps itself aloof from us—I have always been precisely what I have been and what I am at this very moment: who I am and what I am and how and all the rest of it has always been like this. I am here, I am myself, I am nobody else, I have my own as each of us has his own: body, heritage, sleep, meaning, style, character, truth, and if you like complications, untruth, unreality, unbeing and so on, simultaneously with the opposites of them—and there has not been, ever, any full deliverance from death, not the possibility of it, but the living reality of it in the very midst of the living reality of its opposite, everything I have just mentioned, and that is precisely how it is this instant, in Paris, on Thursday, the 26th of June, 1980, as I sip tea and stand at the typewriter and write these words which now either an actor is speaking or a reader, yourself, is reading.

William Saroyan was not known for complaining about physical discomforts. He was deaf in one ear and let everyone know that was why he usually spoke so loud. Several times he has written that he was usually a bit ill, which he considered a normal condition of life. He suffered from an ulcer, and family and friends believed it to be the source of his discomfort in the last years. Even his close cousin, San Francisco writer and painter Archie Minasian, did not know he had cancer until Saroyan collapsed in his Fresno home Sunday night or Monday morning April 20, 1980, the day cousin Ruben Saroyan found him and had him rushed to the hospital. In the previous fall, in September and October, he told me he was sick, but never mentioned cancer. He led me to believe that it was an internal problem, ulcers or digestion, which was the reason for his making elaborate plans for his estate and the William Saroyan Foundation he had established years before. It was because of an ominous premonition, I thought, that he asked me to help arrange the meeting with California State University, Fresno officials in October 1980 to sign a new will to which I was a witness-signatory.

INTRODUCTION

Who knew about the cancer? Almost no one. Even his older brother Henry said during an interview recorded in Lee and Gifford's biography (p.308), "I talked to him during the initial stages, but I did not know that he had cancer of the prostate. He went to the University of California [in San Francisco], to a mutual friend of ours, and I was never told what the diagnosis was." Doctors and nurses, essentially those in contact with Saroyan during the discovery and early treatment of his illness, knew. His Fresno physician was Artin Jibilian, who in the play appears as another facet of the Devil in Act One, Scene 3: "...the shy silent intelligent Armenian born in Alexandria, oh I suppose 40 years or so ago." Saroyan was right about age and other details. Dr. Jibilian is a urologist. He was born and educated in Cairo of Armenian parents. He finished medical school at Cairo University, a faculty where instruction was in English. Internship and residencies were done in Detroit after immigration to the U.S. in 1967. Upon finishing service in the U.S. Army and enjoying a fellowship in urology at the Mayo Clinic, he set up private practice in Fresno in 1975. One of his children is named Aram; this pleased Saroyan a lot.

I have on several occasions spoken to Artin Jibilian about Saroyan's illness and the good doctor sent me the following account in a personal letter dated July 10, 1990.

> My first encounter with Saroyan was in the latter part of October 1979 when he was in urinary retention. After taking care of the immediate problem I explained that he needed surgery. As you know, he had a keen interest in details, therefore, the operation was described and scheduled as soon as possible which was not soon enough for Saroyan. The operation was done on October 27, 1979. The cancer was not diagnosed with the operation, but his prostate felt suspicious. I was almost certain but I wanted to confirm. At this point he refused any further tests, biopsy or scan. He did not want to know, stating that it did not matter because even if he had cancer he would not go along with any treatment for it. He gave a distinct impression that he would accept cancer and that if it would cause his death that is his

destiny and [he] would not prolong or change the course by an artificial means.

Asked about the advice and medication he gave Saroyan before his trip to Eastern Europe, Dr. Jibilian replied, "He was very particular about details, even in his last days he would inquire about the name of the medication from the nurse and turn around and ask [his cousin] Ruben [Saroyan] to write it down for him. I think the medication I gave Saroyan in the summer of 1980 was Darvon or Darvacet." Gail Sarkisian, a nurse at the Veteran's Hospital and a friend of Saroyan's, who was among those attending him during his final illness, reported to me just after his death that in the summer of 1980 she had a phone conversation with him while he was still in Paris in which the writer complained of stomach pains and asked what to do. She also added that on February 22, 1980, nearly three months before a strenuous one month tour of five East European countries, Saroyan found out that he did have cancer.

Those close to Saroyan have often asked why he chose to struggle with willfulness as his only weapon against cancer of the prostate rather than undergo what has been described as a common operation with a very high rate of success if caught in the early stages. The late Archie Minasian, in conversations about this question while he was a guest on our campus during the October 1981 Saroyan Memorial Festival at Fresno State, said that it was a form of suicide, "Bill committed suicide." This seems very uncharacteristic of Saroyan and nowhere in the published or unpublished material that I have so far been able to read is there any concrete evidence of a deliberate letting go.

But Saroyan's life was harder than most people imagine. It was focused entirely upon work. Every day was a working day except when he was traveling from one "office" (Fresno) to the other (Paris). Visits to other countries were to acquire more experiential material, to meticulously observe and record names of people and places in order to turn the new experience immediately into literature. When at home, he felt compelled to work at the typewriter and seemed to have little leisure except breaks on his bicycle in Fresno or walking the streets in Paris in between or after long and intense writing sessions. He was literally addicted to writing; he needed it to live and breathe. And there was no way he could escape from its tyranny and the demands writing made on him except by escaping from living. Surely he was conscious of this, and many have thought about it more than once in analyzing his last two years. Perhaps his journals will provide a clearer answer to the why that we all ask.

One must also not forget that Saroyan seemed at peace in the last months of his life, as the various acts of putting his affairs in order demonstrate. He had come to terms with his cancer and his imminent death, otherwise how could he have described his dying in *Warsaw Visitor* without a trace of anger or bitterness? Saroyan's acceptance of the inevitability of dying is further demonstrated in the essay for the *IHT* quoted earlier, written at the end of August just before his return to Fresno:

"All right, it starts and it stops [the struggle of living], and when it stops if you have had some connection with the world in which William Shakespeare was a kind of star, your name is listed in the annual year-end issue of Variety . . . and there you are. Dead. And famous. And clearly a damned fool. (For dying, of course, for not finding a way to go on fighting, for losing the fight, for giving up the body and spirit's use of muscle in tension and opposition.) Or you are an object of pity—you died too soon, you died in a stupid accident, you were shot in the head by a jealous husband, or a jealous wife, . . . son, . . . daughter, . . . stranger. . . . Or if you are not an object of pity, you are something worse that courtesy almost compels a writer not to mention—indifference: You are an objective of indifference: You have died, your name is in Variety's list, and nobody gives a shit."

At the end of *Warsaw Visitor,* Saroyan typically parades all the characters on the stage for a funny series of non sequiturs, one flowing into the next so naturally. Even the Devil enters into the exchange, now apparently visible and audible not just to the writer, but to everybody. The last words of Moustache's final long speech are, "It is the end of this memoir of my visit to Warsaw and my death there, if you like, or anybody's death there, or anywhere else. That is what it comes to, and I feel it is enough, although it is really so little as to be really nothing, man, nothing at all, so you went to Warsaw in your 72nd year and with you went your disease and your pal Old Red Tail and your life, your entire life so far, going on and on but scheduled to stop.''

There is a nobility in this unusual literary exercise of writing while dying and analyzing the process without rancor, regret or sorrow. It is a tour de force because, as a spectator or reader, though surprised by what Saroyan is telling us, wishing like him that it was not true, we are never frightened nor allowed to feel any apprehension as we go on reading. Nearly the opposite occurs: for we experience the transcendental magic, almost redemption, that we have each felt when reading Saroyan's first story, ''The Daring Young Man on the Flying Trapeze,'' at the end of which the young writer dies of hunger in our own time, in our own world callously indifferent to the sacrifice of creation. Yet the writer is saved, and of that we are convinced through Saroyan's art, just as Saroyan saves himself the same way in *Warsaw Visitor.* That is the creative magic Saroyan understood so early and reiterated to the end: salvation comes through art which immortalizes being.

A wide-angle view of William Saroyan's study-working room, 74 rue Taitbout, Paris with entry and front door to left: in front of the mantle, the desk with chair where he did his business correspondence; to the right the architect's drafting board where he typed his literary works standing up. Below, Saroyan's "new" Royal 800 with a view of the balcony and the rue Taitbout. The room is as he left it for the last time in August 1980. (Photos Dickran Kouymjian)

The back of the new Royal with a silver plaque engraved with his signature and the date August 31, 1960. It was a present he offered himself on his 52nd birthday a few months after he bought his Paris flat. He preferred however, to use his old Royal, though in July 1980 the new one came back into service when the old one broke down. (Photo Dickran Kouymjian)

William Saroyan in front of the Royal typewriter in his Paris apartment, 1974. (Photo Ara Güler)

William Saroyan on the balcony of his fifth floor apartment in Paris, mid-1970s.
(Photo Dickran Kouymjian)

Saroyan's balcony facing north as it looked at the time of his death in the spring of 1981, but as he left it in 1980. The stones were collected during different voyages. The branches used for walking sticks are like the one described in *Warsaw Visitor*. The pots were for his herb garden. (Photo Dickran Kouymjian)

The most recent acquisitions to the stone collection can be seen to the left of the balcony in the upper photo and in a close-up shot below. These pieces of gravestones inscribed in Hebrew and Cyrillic were souvenirs from the Jewish Cemetery in Warsaw that Saroyan brought back to Paris in June 1980. (Photos Dickran Kouymjian)

William Saroyan in 1974 on his Paris balcony holding one of his precious stone-souvenirs. (Photo Ara Güler)

William Saroyan in the front yard of one of his two adjacent Fresno homes at 2729 West Griffith Way on October 21, 1980, the day of the signing of the first of a series of three last wills. (Photo Dickran Kouymjian)

William Saroyan in his second Fresno home at 2739 West Griffith Way on April 11, 1981 reading over his very last will while his cousin Harry Bagdasarian looks on. A week later he was hospitalized. (Photo CSUF Armenian Studies Program Archives)

WILLIAM SAROYAN
1908 -- 1981
ECRIVAIN AMÉRICAIN
D'ORIGINE ARMÉNIENNE
A HABITÉ CET IMMEUBLE
DE 1960 À 1981

The memorial plaque with the inscription "William Saroyan (1908-1981) American writer of Armenian origin lived in this building from 1960 to 1981," placed on the facade of 74 rue Taitbout, Paris, on February 15, 1985, thanks to the efforts of his Paris lawyer Aram Kevorkian. Below, the French masons who mounted the plaque. (Photos Dickran Kouymjian)

Tales from the Vienna Streets

Between the writing of his last two plays Saroyan went to Vienna for the world premiere of his "Play Things" at Vienna's English Theatre scheduled for June 29. It was a fast trip. From an inscription on a book he bought in Vienna, we know he arrived in the Austrian capital on June 28 after completing *Warsaw Visitor* the afternoon before, and was back in Paris on the morning of July 1.

"Play Things" and Vienna's English Theatre

A fortnight earlier, on the 16th of June, the same day Saroyan began to write *Warsaw Visitor,* he made some additions to "Play Things," originally entitled "One Thing and Another." When in 1978 he was invited by the Director of Vienna's English Theatre, Franz Schafranek, to join the famous list of Americans— Edgar Lee Masters, Dorothy Parker, Tennessee Williams, Thornton Wilder, Neil Simon—whose works had been performed at the Theatre, Saroyan obliged with "Play Things," subtitled for the production, "A Theatrical Lark."

Produced by Schafranek, the play was directed by Swedish actress, film director, and writer Mai Zetterling with sets by the pop artist Andy Warhol (1928-1987). In a series of scenes with titles like "Lion's Head and Bear Skin" and "Cup and Saucer," inanimate objects familiar to everybody take on life to argue and discuss a variety of problems and paradoxes. In a letter to Schafranek, quoted in the program, Saroyan offered suggestions for mounting the play: "...bright lights, color, earnestness, absurdity, childishness, health, amusement, intelligence." The play remains unpublished, but will appear in a later volume in this series.

Vienna's English Theatre was founded in 1963 by Ruth Brinkmann, an American actress, with her Austrian actor-director husband Franz Schafranek. For years it has had the distinction of being the only full time, fully professional English language theater in continental Europe. It has been housed since 1975 in a splendid neo-Baroque theater built in 1905-6 in Vienna's Josefsgasse. In addition to Saroyan's "Play Things' it has also mounted world premieres of works by Tennessee Williams and more recently Edward Albee, and offered a wide repertory of twentieth century British and American classics.

It was not Saroyan's first Vienna premiere. On February 17, 1960, his *The Dogs, or The Paris Comedy,* a play written in Paris in August 1959, while his children Aram and Lucy were living with him in a rented flat had its first performance and then went on to West Germany. It was published ten years later in New York in a volume entitled *The Dogs, or The Paris Comedy and Two Other Plays: Chris Sick, or Happy New Year Anyway, Making Money and 19 Other Very Short Plays.* 1959, the year after he left forever his home on the beach at Malibu was a busy time for Saroyan, for on March 12 his most surrealist play, *Jim Dandy, Fat Man in a Famine,* written before the World War, but published and first performed in 1947, had its Philadelphia premiere. Early in *Warsaw Visitor* Moustache offers proof to Ms. Rye of his fluency in German by relating that he once said to film director George Stevens, "Nein, nein, Jim Dandy ist Jim Dandy," and by pronouncing Jim Dandy, "Shim Tdanty."

During the Vienna trips, Saroyan, as was his custom, explored the city, interested in everybody and everything. Daily he went to the Griechenbeisl, one of Vienna's best known and oldest traditional restaurants, already famous in the fifteenth century. Retired California Superior Court Judge Spurgeon Avakian reported in a letter of July 31, 1987 to Ben Amirkhanian, Director of Fresno's annual Saroyan Festival, how he and his wife sat at a table in the restaurant with Saroyan's picture on the wall above it. "The waiter told us that. . . Saroyan went there daily, for coffee and conversation. . . whenever he was in Vienna."

After the premiere of "Play Things," the production and direction of which Saroyan liked very much, Schafranek asked Saroyan to write a play especially for his theater. Saroyan agreed and asked that Mai Zetterling also direct it, since he was so pleased by her approach to "Play Things." Two weeks after his last trip, on Thursday afternoon July 17, 1980, he began *Tales from the Vienna Streets,* "a play, ballet, opera, etcetera etcetera," as he indicated on page one. He later crossed out all but "a play." Exactly a week later on Wednesday the 23rd he had finished it, though the next day he added an addendum with clarifications and some additional stage directions. Again he began with his usual habit of completing one 800 word page on the first day, on the second he wrote two, and for the next five days, three pages each in continuous sessions. His speed in composing had declined: an average of thirty-eight minutes per page for the eighteen pages of the play as compared to the more characteristic twenty-eight minutes per page for the thirty-three pages of *Warsaw Visitor,* of which eighteen pages were written in less than half an hour. Only one page of *Tales* was written in less than thirty minutes, and three pages demanded more than fifty minutes, an extremely slow pace for Saroyan. Why? Was he fatigued or suffering from his cancer? Was he not sure of where the play was going? Did he allow interruptions—answering the telephone for example?

Franz Schafranek kept in contact with Saroyan about the new play and its logical premiere in Vienna's English Theatre. A short time after completing the play, Saroyan carefully edited it with pen on the original typescript, as was his custom, had several photocopies made, and mailed one to Schafranek on July 29, 1980. According to the latter, he visited Saroyan in Paris in August "to finish collaboration" on the production of the play, but the work was "still incomplete when Saroyan left for Fresno." Schafranek contacted him once in Fresno, "but the work remained incomplete when Saroyan died." This information was reported to me orally by Schafranek himself on July 31 of this year (1990), yet nine years earlier to the day, six weeks after Saroyan's death, Thomas Quinn Curtiss, the veteran theater critic of the *International Herald Tribune,* published a piece in the *IHT* (July 31, 1981) entitled: "Saroyan's 'Tales' Due for Vienna Premiere."

In this preview Curtiss discussed aspects of the play in such detail that he most certainly had access to the typescript. He was precise about the production, ". . . the play, not yet published, is scheduled for its premiere next season [that is 1981-82] at Vienna's English Theatre." Saroyan, in the fall of 1980, never talked about a future production of this play with me, but the copy of the typescript I was given can be considered a completed one, as finished as any of the dozens of plays in manuscript that I have examined, and among them the only one with such detailed stage directions. There can be no doubt that Saroyan thought of a Vienna production from the first moment of the play's composition, otherwise no character descriptions or staging indications would have made their way into the original writing.

Most of the plays of his last twenty years—there are more than one hundred—were written by Saroyan with no thought of their immediate production. He talks about this over and over again in letters and published memoirs. "In 1943 I turned my back on Broadway, but I did not stop writing plays. I simply stopped offering my plays to the machine that was huffing and puffing in the business of getting plays on the boards in front of New Yorkers and people from out of town who had money to spend on tickets. I wrote new plays every year, I have the plays, and they *do* constitute my theatre, and they are part of the real American theatre, and of the real world theatre, even though they have not been produced, performed, and witnessed." (*Here Comes There Goes You Know Who,* p.224.) The same theme but with more elaboration is frolicked with in "How to Write a Great Play," published by *TV Guide,* March 6, 1976:

> The way to write a great play is the same as the way to write a poor play. What you do is get the materials and objects needed for any kind of writing: paper, typewriter, pen or pencil. And you use these materials and objects in the writing of whatever it is that you want to write.... Traditionally, plays gets performed, but only if the playwright insists on it, as most of the famous American playwrights do, and only if the playwrights are willing to put up with the hocus-pocus of the theater, and for years I haven't been willing. But that doesn't mean that I don't write plays. I write new plays every year, because writing is my work and I prefer work to idleness.... It is too much bother of a boring nature to fight with the money, and the real estate, and the national art councils, and the foundations, to get a play on the boards— never mind the unions and the Mafiosi of success and failure of the Great White Way.... I write plays out of the madness that has come into my life from early bookreading and

continuous involvement with the anonymous but immortal human race in Fresno, San Francisco, New York, Paris and the cities and towns of the rest of the world that I knew. He concludes by answering the original question, "The way to write a great play is to be great, isn't it? The way to write a poor play is to be thinking of getting rich."

Not only was Vienna's English Theatre ready to produce *Tales from the Vienna Streets* in the 1981-82 season, but Mai Zetterling and Andy Warhol were ready to collaborate on it. Dr. Schafranek, in the same personal conversation already referred to, said, "When I told Andy Warhol about the possibility of doing *Tales*, he was excited and said 'sensational, I'll be happy to do it. Send me word when it is ready.'" Schafranek even contacted the Kennedy Center for the Performing Arts in Washington about a co-production. "They were very excited and even wanted to mount an exhibition on Saroyan to coincide with the opening." Furthermore, Schafranek continued, "I contacted Elia Kazan, Saroyan's contemporary in age, to direct the play, but he said he had stopped directing, adding that he liked Saroyan a lot and was flattered by the offer."

The play, however, was never produced in that season, nor after. Schafranek maintains the collaboration was not completed, yet the play was scheduled for a coming production and so publicized months after Saroyan's death. Was it a question of permission? Was it an overly ambitious project? For the moment I do not know the answer.

Tales and Saroyan's Vienna

Tales from the Vienna Streets is ready for production. Of the typescripts of unpublished Saroyan plays that I have examined closely, only those composed with a specific production or publication in mind were graced with indications of settings or descriptions of characters such as we find in *Tales*. Furthermore, the play was edited and revised by Saroyan before he sent it to Vienna. The same was true of *Armenians,* performed in New York, in 1975, published in the first volume of this series, *William Saroyan: An Armenian Trilogy.* Saroyan's editing of the original

Tales typescript for production in Vienna resulted in cutting back extra language and clarifying the action. In my own editing of the play for publication, I have respected completely Saroyan's changes even when the original was better than the rewrite. A few typos were corrected and I changed the spelling of one word: "gaz" to gas, used many times in the play, even though I know Saroyan probably wanted the European and Armenian way of writing and pronouncing it for added humor. As was often the case with early Saroyan scripts, his most important changes were made in the opening and the finale of the play.

Tales from the Vienna Streets takes place in a public setting as in so many of his previous talk plays, where diverse representatives of society can interact with each other. In *The Time of Your Life* (1939) it was Nick's Pacific Street Saloon, Restaurant and Entertainment Palace in San Francisco, in *Jim Dandy, Fat Man in a Famine* (1941, published 1947) it was the ruins of a public library, in *The Oyster and the Pearl* (1953) a barbershop in OK-by-the-Sea, California, in *The Cave Dwellers* (performed 1957, published 1958) an abandoned theater in New York City, in *Sam, The Highest Jumper of Them All* (1960 performance, 1961 publication) it was a bank in London, in *Armenians* (1971, performance 1975, publication 1986) the Holy Trinity Armenian Church and the Asbarez Club in Fresno, *Haratch* (1979, published 1986) it was the editorial offices of the Armenian daily in Paris. For this, "Saroyan's last work for the theater," according to Thomas Quinn Curtiss's preview, Saroyan returned to a cafe, the environment of his first great Pulitzer Prize-winning success, *The Time of Your Life.*

The Armenian Connection

The Haydakor Coffee House in Vienna does not exist, nor is there, to the best of my knowledge, such an establishment in that city operated or owned by Armenians as in the play. Though coffee as a drink was introduced into Europe—specifically Vienna and Paris—in the seventeenth century by Armenian merchants, a fact that Saroyan was surely aware of because of his fondness for trivial knowledge in general and Armenian trivia in particular, his countrymen have not in modern times been active as cafe or restaurant proprietors.

The name Haydakor is itself a curious one; Curtiss for instance fails to cite it, because he could not have penetrated its meaning. Saroyan coined it from the word Armenians use in their own language to designate themselves, "Hay" ("Armenian," pronounced "hi") and the French word for O.K., "d'accord" (orally the final "d" is unpronounced and the double "c" sounds like "k"). Haydakor's meaning is thus clear: "Armenian, O.K." It is not the first time O.K. was used to name a Saroyan environment. Already in the TV play *The Oyster and the Pearl,* written for Alastair Cooke's Omnibus Show, the town was called OK-by-the-Sea. Saroyan also used it on other occasions. In Scene 14 of *Tales,* Alfie, the Boy, says to the Girl, "Why did we *come* here?" to which she replies, "We came here for luck, don't you remember? You said somebody you know told you that going to the Haydakor Coffee House brings a person good luck."

A few words of explanation are in order for other specifically Armenian terminology. The play begins whimsically with the following curious dialogue, "Van: Hayek, Bahrone? Schmidt: Alec? Aroon? Who is Alec Aroon?" Saroyan wanted the audience to perceive slowly that for Schmidt, a non-Armenian, the word "Hayek" sounds like Alec because of the last syllable, and Aroon like the Armenian "Bahrone," which Schmidt also failed to grasp. Throughout *Tales* there is a play on the name Alec Aroon, a fictitious character even in the work, only explained at the very end. When Armenians, especially those living in the widespread diaspora that is part of their modern condition, think they are by chance in the presence of another Armenian, or suspect or hope that they are, they ask discreetly: "Hay ek," literally, "Armenian, are you?" (with the polite plural form of the verb), followed by "Bahrone," "Sir" from the old French title Baron, which entered Armenian in the twelfth century when the Crusaders and the Armenians were allies. Saroyan often spelled Armenian words in a way that would guarantee authentic pronunciation in American English, as for instance the special guide appended to the performing version of *My Heart's in the Highlands* with specific

31

instructions on how to say the Armenian used by Johnny's grandmother. For the example to hand, he also could have indicated proper pronunciation by spelling it "Bar-own."

The Armenian composer-conductor Loris Tjeknavorian, Saroyan's choice for composing the music in the play, spent his early years in Iran. During the 1970s and 1980s he held posts in London and America. His recordings include his own compositions and the classics, for instance the complete symphonies of Aleksandr Borodin. Last year he was appointed Director of the Armenian Philharmonic in Erevan and recently toured the U.S.—Boston, New York and Los Angeles—with the orchestra.

Van and Ho speak often in the play about the Mekhitarist Congregation, Armenian monks of Catholic persuasion, but totally nationalist in sentiment. The Congregation has one of its two major centers in Vienna. Saroyan, like most of his countrymen, had a fondness for these fathers, who for nearly three centuries have led the intellectual revival of the nation through their ambitious program of Armenian language publications. The Order was started by Mekhitar of Sebastia (1676-1749) who, after fleeing religious persecution in the Ottoman Empire, found refuge for himself and his young pupils in Venice. In 1717 the Doge gave the monks the abandoned island of San Lazzaro (Saint Lazarus), a medieval leper colony located in the Venice lagoon, where the Congregation's headquarters and famous printing presses were established. In 1811 a group of dissident priests, who separated from the Order in 1773, finally established themselves in Vienna. Their monastery-museum-library-school-printing house, the Mekhitaristen Kloster, is located on Mekhitaristengasse, just behind Museum Strasse, in the center of Vienna. The Mekhitarist school that the owners of the Haydakor Coffee House send their young relatives to is one of many educational establishments operated by the two branches of the Congregation throughout the Armenian diaspora.

The Graben, a popular tourist and shopping street in the heart of the old town, where Saroyan situates the Haydakor Coffee House in the play, and the neighboring St. Stephens Cathedral, are a short twenty minute walk from Mekhitarist Monastery toward the Danube. Saroyan knew the area well from his various visits, thus accounting for the usual authenticity of environment associated with his works.

Plot, Structure, and Characters

Each of the eighteen scenes of *Tales from the Vienna Streets* begins with some entertainment—singing, dancing, pantomime— recalling the various acts and sketches Saroyan used in *The Time of Your Life*—in the original unedited typescript, the Boy and the Girl were to be young ballet dancers. The clowning and antics are once again reminiscent of vaudeville, which had such a marked influence on the young Saroyan, one that he never failed to acknowledge. But this play is not *The Time of Your Life* in a 1980s setting, even though Schmidt's offering of coffee to the Boy and Girl is reminiscent of Joe's sharing of champagne with Kitty and others; and Alice in one of her earlier incarnations was a streetwalker, like some of the women who come and go in *The Time of Your Life*. Even Joe's famous line in Act Two, "It takes a lot of rehearsing for a man to get to be himself." is by Alice in *Tales* while reading a coffee cup in Scene 10: "A man has got to give his performance. Woe unto the man who has not rehearsed." Though the Haydakor may bring good fortune to its habitues, like Nick's place did to Kitty and others, it is not the symbolic refuge for society's outsiders who, within its confines, find a magical wholeness as they did in the San Francisco bar.

The song and dance routines of the play are more like those Saroyan had intended for his very first play, *Subway Circus,* written in New York in 1935, after he found out from the *New York Times* that he had written a play. By "not wanting to make a liar out of the New York *Times*," he wrote *Subway Circus* a few days before booking passage to Europe and Armenia for the first time. The subtitle of the play in its printed version (*Razzle-Dazzle,* 1942) was "A Vaudeville." An introduction accompanied the text in which Saroyan links the play to a trip to the circus in New York's Madison Square Garden with Carl Sandburg. The work is made up of ten sketches which include dancing, singing, mime, acrobatics, and dialogue. Yet whereas the staging of *Subway Circus* is similar to *Tales from the Vienna Streets,* the action is not. *Tales* has a plot.

True to Saroyan's own ideals about theater, the plot of the Vienna play is a loose one. It was not his custom—he was indeed vociferous about this point—to use plot or suspense or action as the driving forces of his theater. Situation, and especially language and ideas discussed, are the essentials of this and so many other Saroyan works.

The cast includes in addition to the proprietor of the Haydakor Coffee House, Van Vaspouraganian (the last name being a play on the first, since the city of Van on the Lake of the same name, now in modern Turkey, is situated in the ancient Armenian province of Vaspouragan) and his cousin Hovakim, both of whom are realistically portrayed. In addition there are four major figures, all of them archetypal. The mature adults, Schmidt and Alice, represent man and woman over the centuries, each of them alluding from time to time to incarnations from earlier times. The Boy and the Girl represent young adults of our time. She, who has no name in the play, but who Saroyan in the addendum suggests may be called Anna, is "the very daughter of the human race, . . . the mother who is forever sought by the father." Despite this description, she is more a naive innocent than a universal figure. Alfie, the Boy, is "a son of the human race, but apparently with dominant female reality, and aspirations for motherhood instead of fatherhood."

In the previous pages these plays have been discussed in terms of their origins, their mode of construction, and Saroyan's particular situation while he was creating them. In conclusion I should like to assess them as works of art.

Warsaw Visitor and *Tales from the Vienna Streets:* Two Parts of a Whole

Always when the ancients went in search of God they traveled East. By fate, fortune, or foreknowledge, Saroyan's voyage to the

East, the very cradle of those ancients, was the source and motivation of his last two plays. Written swiftly and almost simultaneously and inspired by the two key waystops on his journey, their interrelationship seems inevitable.

To begin with, they share an uncommon dramatic feature: the use of an "outside" narrator, a kind of off-stage commentator who apprises the audience of goings on. In *Warsaw Visitor* he is Saroyan himself, stepping forward to introduce characters, to describe the course of his illness, and to dazzle us with art as paradox. In *Tales from the Vienna Streets* he is Van, standing aloof from the action and describing it objectively until almost the end of the play, when shortly after Alfie dies Ho tells us: "Van has accepted a part in the play." Key phrases too recur in both the plays, the most notable being "Sir, I say Sir," almost a refrain in *Warsaw Visitor* and popping up unexpectedly in *Tales from the Vienna Streets* as though to point a finger at its counterpart.

The meaning of the two plays actually underlines their relationship. I mentioned earlier how in *Warsaw Visitor* Saroyan delves deep into the meaning of life and death and how the characters in *Tales from the Vienna Streets* are archetypal. The themes of both plays are therefore vast, perhaps the broadest in scope of any of Saroyan's works. And the timeless central motif of each is established by the character of the city in which the play is set.

"Warsaw means Jews." Saroyan as Moustache tells us near the end of *Warsaw Visitor,* having made it clear earlier in the play that by Jews he also means Armenians, Africans, and Asians—minorities set apart, in isolation. Warsaw, pulling back from Russia and alien to Western Europe, is also set apart, in isolation. And Saroyan, a writer traveling with, but set apart from, his fellows, and further isolated by the immanence of death, becomes the individual embodiment of Warsaw. Moreover his self, his alter ego, and his shadow side (the Devil) face his own death march with the courage of persecuted minorities everywhere; the drama of their living and dying parallels his own. "We are fragile and can go, can be taken at any moment," he tells us, "but as long as we are not taken we are without doubt one of the most enduring orders of substances and actions that may exist or might be imagined as existing in the world, on earth, in the universe.''

If Warsaw is unique unto itself, Vienna has ''settled dead center in the heart of all of the great cities of the world: Paris, Berlin, Moscow, Rome, Madrid, London, New York, San Francisco.'' If Warsaw is isolation, Vienna is the world. In *Warsaw Visitor* minorities are a race apart. In *Tales from the Vienna Streets,* they are the ''keepers of secrets:.... gypsies, Jews, farmers, bankers, garbage-collectors, lawyers, accountants, floor-walkers, doctors, and Armenians.'' We are all of us minorities, minorities of one, each sharing with our private devil the guilt and innocence of humanity.

In *Tales* Saroyan moves from the individual to the collective through clearly archetypal characters. His language is replete with biblical allusions: the birth of a child, three wise men, and over and over the mention of a savior. The Haydakor Coffee House is also archetypal. It is the locus of idyllic tranquillity, the original Garden of Paradise, as so many references and situations in the play make clear. It may be that behind Saroyan's character the Guarden Offizier is not a lapsus for the German Gardeoffizier, Officer of the Guards, but rather for Gartenoffizier, Officer of the Garden.

In this archetypal Garden the most timeless drama of them all takes place. Alfie, husband and wife, father and mother, man and woman alike, ''a male child from about 30 years ago went berserk in the soul and dropped dead.'' In this culminating moment of the play we have the Fall of Man, of humankind, in Haydakor, Saroyan's Garden of Eden. Yet in *Tales* as in *Warsaw Visitor* death is not the end. Alfie died while striving to create, striving to perpetuate the human race. In recognition of this, Van accepts the part of ''Father'' (capital letter, Saroyan's) in the play. Our Father enters the Garden and restores it to life while Ho—Hovakim, St. Joachim, father of Mary—prepares the Cafe-Garden ''for tomorrow.'' Then ''very slowly the lights go out and something like a dazzling sky full of childhood's galaxies of stars seems to be where the scene had been.''

INTRODUCTION

In *Warsaw Visitor* the individual prevails in the face of death, the Dying Old Man on the Flying Trapeze leaps off into the unknown one final time, open-eyed and unafraid. In *Tales from the Vienna Streets* all humankind, creative and striving, dies and yet lives on to create and strive again, open-eyed and unafraid. "The play goes on," Saroyan tells us, for him, and them, and all of us.

WARSAW VISITOR

A Play in Two Acts

Portraits of William Saroyan during his last East European trip, May 1980. Below, with his Polish interpreter named "Martha Mularuk" in *Warsaw Visitor*. (Photos Dickran Kouymjian)

Photographs of Saroyan in Warsaw during a panel discussion by American writers at the University of Warsaw, May 16, 1980, novelist Joyce Carol Oates on the right. (Photos Ryszard Dutkiewicz)

William Saroyan at the reception held at the University of Warsaw after an American writers' panel, May 16, 1980. (Photos Dickran Kouymjian)

William Saroyan talking with a group of young writers and students during his trip to Eastern Europe. (Photos Dickran Kouymjian)

William Saroyan with a scythe showing off his farming skills in May 1980 while his Polish interpreter in *Warsaw Visitor*, ''Martha Mularuk,'' looks on amused. (Photos Dickran Kouymjian)

William Saroyan visiting the Jewish Cemetery in Warsaw, May 26, 1980. (Photos Włodzimierz Przybył)

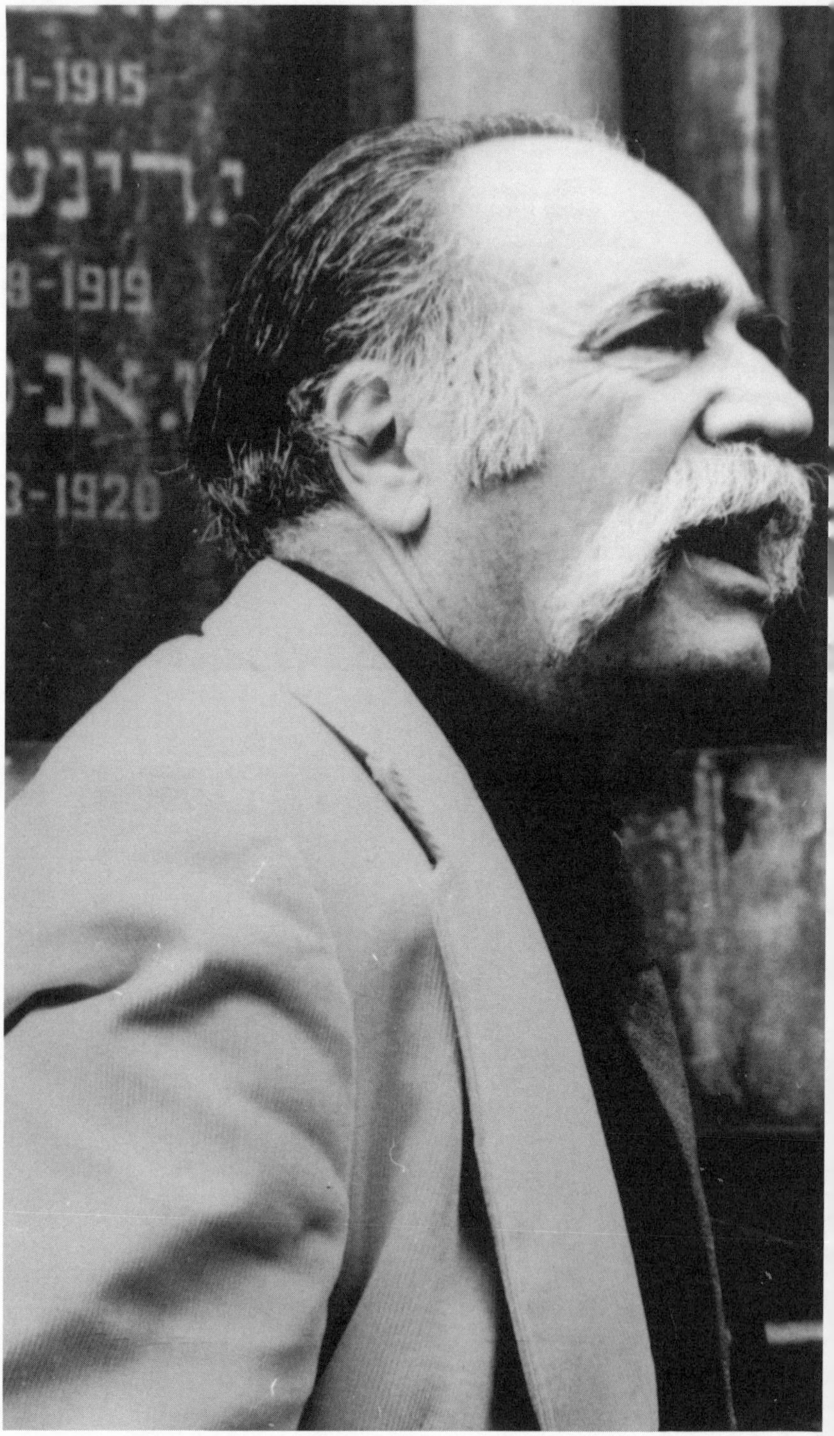

William Saroyan visiting the Jewish Cemetery in Warsaw, May 26, 1980, an episode described in detail in *Warsaw Visitor*. (Photos Włodzimierz Przybyf)

William Saroyan at the end of his visit to the Jewish Cemetery in Warsaw, May 26, 1980. (Photos Wlodzimierz Przybyl)

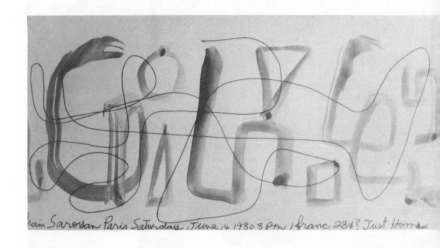

Drawings Saroyan made into newly purchased 25¢ books. Dated June 14, 1980 they celebrate his arrival in Paris from Eastern Europe with the title "Just Home." (Photos Dickran Kouymjian)

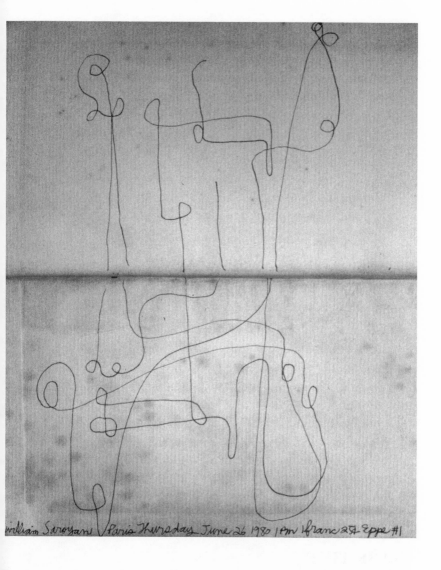

william Saroyan / Paris Thursday June 26 1980 1 pm 1 franc 25 Eppe #1

Drawing dated "June 26 1980 1 pm," in a 25¢ book bought and inscribed between the first and second writing sessions on *Warsaw Visitor* during the day before he finished it. (Photo Dickran Kouymjian)

THE PEOPLE

THE DEVIL, *also appears briefly as* MOUSTACHE'S *doctor*

MOUSTACHE, *72 years old, American-Armenian writer,* SAROYAN *as a character in the play*

VOICE, MOUSTACHE'S *subconscious while dreaming*

DANIEL LISH, *American writer*

MS ELENA RYE, wife of DANIEL LISH

MARTHA MULARUK, *22 years old,* MOUSTACHE'S *official Polish interpreter in Warsaw*

ALAN SCHNEIDER, *American producer-director*

SAROYAN, *author of the play as commentator*

WOMAN, *in audience*

MAN, *in audience*

BUDDINGTON, *American poet*

ROGER DEVONSHIRE, *Chief Cultural Officer, American Embassy, Warsaw*

CARETAKER, *Jewish Cemetery in Warsaw*

SECOND WOMAN, *employee in Lenin Museum of Poland*

THE PLACE

Hotel in Mainz, and Frankfurt airport, in Germany.
Hotel Europejski, residence of the American Ambassador, a conference hall, P.E.N. Club, a limousine, Jewish Theatre, Chopin's birthplace, American Embassy, Jewish Cemetery, a street, Lenin Museum of Poland, Jewish Museum, all in Warsaw.
Saroyan's apartment in Paris.

THE TIME

Mid-May 1980

NOTE: The play was written without acts or scenes in Paris between June 16 and 17, 1980. It has been divided into two acts with twelve scenes by the editor.

I Have Seen the Future, and It Works.
Lincoln Steffens, 1929

I Have Seen Everything. And Nothing Works.
William Saroyan, 1980

ACT ONE

PROLOGUE

MAN COSTUMED LIKE THE LEGENDARY DEVIL, WITH HORNS AND TAIL
Why are you standing there, operating that infernal machine?

MAN WITH LARGE WHITE MOUSTACHE
Ho, what a question. Sir, I say Sir, this infernal machine is a
typewriter, and it works. It is one of the few things left in the
world that does work. And I Sir, I say Sir, again and again I
want it understood that I speak to everybody, including yourself,
Sir, with respect, and frequently with affection, or at any rate
sympathy. Back to the question, then: why am I standing here
operating this machine. Sir, I say Sir, I am a writer and I am
writing my memoirs.

DEVIL
Oh, fiddlesticks, oh, fie, oh fie—your memoirs? What have you
got to remember? And when you have written your memoirs,
what then? I mean, arrogant old man pretending to be courteous
and humble with a very sharp customer, what then? What then?
So you write your memoirs, so what then? I mean, surely you
might be out in the country walking along a sweet path among
all manner of growth and greenery, might you not?

MOUSTACHE

I might, indeed I might, but I came to a time sixty years ago
when I had to decide if I was to live an unnoticed life or if I
was to notice whatever might be said to be my portion, my life.
I decided in favor of art, but Sir, I say Sir, let me remind you
that having chosen art I did not relinquish life, or forfeit it, and
soon enough art and life were the same, and I went everywhere
and saw everybody and everything and came home to myself
and this infernal machine as you put it and put down in simple
words what I had seen and heard. And all of the rest of it. And
you, and you, Sir, I say Sir, what are you doing there back
of where I stand, always in the back of me, in the back of all of
us, if this is anything at all like the language this question
deserves? Why do you hover about with your silly long tail with
its arrow-pointed end and with your really ridiculous horns.
Who are you to have horns and just what do they signify, pray
tell, Sir, I say Sir, what does your red underwear signify, are
you a joke, a mockery of the sincere feeling in all honorable
men, women and children that it is possible to live a good life?
Are you laughing at us as we mosey along, mosey along, day
after long day, long long day after long long long day? Pray
tell. I mean, Sir, I say Sir, why do you hang back there that way?

DEVIL

Do not ask a silly question and you will not be given a rude
reply. You know more about this than you pretend. And so you
stand there and work the infernal machine, making neat words
strung together into neat sentences and finally your memoirs
are written, so what then, what then?

MOUSTACHE

I write them again.

DEVIL

Oh, no, no, this is going too far. There was nothing to remember
and you remembered it and then you went to work at that infernal

machine and you remembered and wrote the whole thing all
over again. Why?

MOUSTACHE

Sorrow. Sympathy. You perhaps are not moved when you hear
strange sounds out of the bodies, the lungs, the mouths of human
beings, but I am, I am terribly moved when I hear an old husband
and wife talking softly about the long past, the kids grown up
and gone into the manufacture of new kids, their own terrible
kids, named and carefully noticed, special at birth, and ever
afterwards an awful mystery. Because I must. Because I am
here. Because I still have health enough for it. Because the illness
packaged into me at birth, the disease of life, compels me to
do so, although by God let us try not to forget that there was
a day in my soul when to be a fireman at a big fire, leaping
off a red wagon and fixing the mighty fire-hose to the fire-
hydrant and holding the powerful force of the flying water upon
the lovely flames of a magnificent church, let's say, empty of
people, but containing a family of church mice—there was a
day, Sir, I say Sir, when to be that great man, the fireman at
the fire, was the supreme achievement out of all of the
possibilities in the entire human experience. And I didn't see
it through. I worry about the family of church mice.

DEVIL

Sorrow. Sympathy. You're silly, and I suppose you have a name
that has a meaning, perhaps a large meaning in the world, or
at any rate that tiny part of it that might be said to be literary,
is that right?

MOUSTACHE

Yes, it is indeed right, Sir, I say Sir. I have such a name and
I am told that it is one of the great names. And it means me.

DEVIL

It means me, he says. It means nobody. But have your little
fun, as I believe the Americans sometimes put it. You are, are

59

you not, an American, mayhap? I ask because being an American is an amazing piece of absurdity, you know, and there is this absurdity in yourself, with the big white moustache. The only Americans are the local Indians and they are Asiatics of various kinds who walked on the frozen water from around Kamchatka over the Bering Straits to the continent of North America—I wish, I wish, Lord Lord Lord how I wish the information were just an edge less boring, but there it is, we of Heaven as you of Earth have no real control over the information and so it becomes a matter of take it or leave it. Do you take the information, or do you leave it?

MOUSTACHE

Oh, I don't know, I don't really have much, I don't go by the general information, at any rate, but I am unable not to notice that when I glanced at you a moment ago I saw, or thought I saw, that you wore a moustache precisely like my own, and I thought, Now, that's very strange, and then I thought again and decided, Now, that's not strange at all, but the moustache is gone, so I know that it was an optical illusion and the miraculous arrival of the illusion as a reality upon your face was not part of the general information, was not part of that which we live by, and I suppose die by, or somewhat die by— if anybody in God's name is listening, this is only that which in baseball is known as warming up, ignore it if you like. I wish I could, but it is me, it is this American, it is this ethnic whoever, I know the theory just fine, but at this moment it does not seem at all crucial to art or life to name it. Saying it is one thing, being it is another—Choctaw, Navajo, Iroquois, whatever the ethnic of the nose and eyes, head and scalp may be. What do you want? I mean, why are you hanging back of me wherever I go, even here in room 78 of the Roomerwall Hotel in Mainz, Germany, West Germany, because there is not one room to be had at any of the great hotels in Frankfurt because for a writer, even with a name, there is never a room at a hotel in Frankfurt because all of the rooms are taken by the pilgrims who visit Frankfurt every day from all over the world—Lord Lord Lord, as he himself said a moment ago, help us help us to find a hotel room in the world at the best hotel in town with a glorious view of the river and forest and the towers of glorious architecture. Do not give all of the rooms to executives of banks, insurance companies, Arabian oil distilleries, government agents of all kinds, and all manner of pert little men holding slick briefcases containing you know what—the formula for the destruction of the world and the human race as well as most of the whales in the sea. The last time I visited Frankfurt there was a Book Fair but again not a room in any hotel, so I had to sleep in Weisbaden which is just across the river from Mainz, because the workingman on the train from Frankfurt to Mainz told me so, coming all the way from Yugoslavia's Sarajevo for the good money—he will go home in a year a rich man with a social disease, or a distaste for farm and village life. Kamchatka? Why Kamchatka? What is the meaning of Kamchatka? Are you sure you have got it right? Do you mean perhaps Chamkatka, Katchamka, Macatchma, or what is the code in operation here? What do you want? Let's get down to the bottom line, as the brisk young fraudulent stupid Americans like to put it, swarming all over the District of Columbia, Manhattan Island, Chicago's Lakeshore, Detroit's bankrupt chainbelt automobile factories, Hollywood's television and movie factories, San Francisco's hillside guru temples—on and on and on, as we say now and then in something like despair. Sir, I say Sir, what do you want? Surely you can see for yourself that all I want is a little sleep after a flight from San Francisco to New York to Frankfurt. Permit me to congratulate you on your costume and make-up, if you were in a silent movie at the Liberty Theatre in Fresno in 1917, by God, I would be delighted by the meaning of your hanging back of everybody and everything, but this is another time and place and all I want to do is get a little sleep. Rocketing about the world in the dragonfly's fuselage gets very tiring you know, never mind what it may be to rocket to the moon. I wouldn't go there even if they had a good room at the best hotel with a view of Lady Godiva still riding the horse bareback in search of—me? Was it me? Just let me sleep, please. I am on a mission that needs the best force within myself that I can summon. Is it a deal, Sir?

DEVIL

You know perfectly well the only deal I make, for it is in all of the legends, poems, stories, plays, operas, and ballets of life.

SCENE 1

VOICE

What's that phone ringing for? I don't have anybody to phone me, do I? **Papa? I just wanted to say I love you.** Who are you? **I am your daughter. Remember? Tumbling Tumbleweed?** Listen here, girl, woman, you are now thirty, you should have had four kids by now, you know I hate the telephone, if you want to tell me something send me a letter, will you? **Oh, Papa, oh, Papa, oh, Papa, I love you just the same, goodbye.** No, no, no, wait, you haven't used up the three minutes you are going to be charged anyway, so—ring ring ring—why do you ring and let the phone company get rich? We've got two full minutes, so why have you called, what's on your mind—you do have a little mind, do you not, little girl? **Oh, Papa, I have a big mind, and you know it, I thought you would want to know that I'm engaged to Racey Dill and he is heavenly, Papa, Racey Dill is the most misunderstood American star of movies since Rudolph Valentino and he is madly in love with me.** Racey Dill did you say, listen, baby, you know Racey Dill is queer, how can you phone to tell me you are engaged to a man who gets himself beat up every weekend by anybody he can manage. **Papa, those are publicity lies, that's what they are, his studio is doing all that sort of thing to force him to break his contract, he is making more money than they are, and he wants me to be his wife and the mother of his children and his secretary and the caretaker of his finances and everything, isn't it exciting?** Listen, little girl, I remember you from birth and this news you

are giving me is not exciting, it is very boring, it is depressing—
at least O'Neill had his Anna Christie walking the streets like
an honorable whore. I don't want to put this sort of thing into
a play—the three minutes are almost up. Listen to me, dear little
girl, find a man, won't you, tell him the truth about yourself,
all of it, and if he will have you, marry him, and have yourselves
a son and a daughter or two of each, and I think the telephone
company will put you in a big full page New York Times ad
remarking how in a phone call to your father your life was
changed—and mind you changed for the better. **Oh, Papa, I
love you, I love Racey Dill, I love the Safeway checkout clerk
you want me to shock with the story of my life and to marry,
and I love the telephone company, goodbye.** — What was
that? And why is the phone still ringing, pray tell. Where am
I? **Hello. Hello. Is that you, old friend?** Hang up, you silly
stupid son of a bitch, I don't know anybody who talks that way.
You've got another wrong number, and you yourself were born
a wrong number and you'll dial wrong numbers the rest of your
stupid life confirming it, now won't you, you silly stupid son
of a bitch. Christ Almighty, a man flies through the air with
the greatest disease and he finally comes down in Hotdog
Heaven, Frankfurter itself, and there isn't a room in town, so
he finds out how to pay for a ticket from a chewing-gum
dispensing machine so he can get out of town forty miles to
Mainz where a room is waiting, and he finally gets himself and
his stupid heavy suitcases and his stupid old typewriter on a
stupid German train and he rolls and rolls with the stupid new
German train and the man is doing all this silly stuff for art
or something, for literature or something, for the human race
or something, the man is an idiot, you know, just like his idiot
daughter, and his idiot son, and he almost passes Mainz because
travelers have told him that Mainz is two more stops but
suddenly a trainman says no, no, sir, this is Mainz, so he lugs
himself and his luggage off the stupid train and finds out where
the taxis wait for fools, and he hauls the luggage like a tired
old horse because there are no such things as porters and he
lugs and lugs and comes to the first of a dozen taxis in a row

and he mentions the name of the hotel: Raemerwall or whatever the hell it is, and the taxi-driver points to a building about 200 yards away, meaning why don't you walk it, and the old fool, tired man tired, says no, drive me there I'm not interested in saving a buck and killing myself, so the heavy suitcase is heaved into the trunk compartment and the typewriter kept beside the old fool of a writer and they go and go and when they go into the driveway of the hotel the meter shows a good big chunk of like money of some kind—two dollars maybe three maybe four with a dollar tip, and then the manager looks it up and says, here it is, room 78, and they walk out of that building to another building and they climb one flight of stairs—hold it, hold it, what am I telling all this stuff for, I'm tired, I'm trying to get to sleep. **Pop? Hey, Pop? How are you? What's going on?** Hoo boy, this time it's the first-born, the son, also a telephone virtuoso. Listen, I'm fine, I want to sleep, write to me someday when the spirit moves you. I've got to sleep now. Goodbye.

MOUSTACHE

Would you say your name once again please, I seem to hear something like Armadillo and I know that can't be it at all, you have the voice of a secretary of some kind, the voice of a young woman of considerable responsibility and ability, but let me make this important suggestion, when you speak on the telephone always presume that the listener has poor hearing, as I do, and always go to the trouble of enunciating the important words very clearly: otherwise the telephone will fail, it will become extinct, like the big animals with long necks and small heads and tiny brains, you see—and of course you will notice that I am enunciating my own words as if you know them as I do, as if you were saying them, and that's another telephone fallacy—strangers by accident on the line mumble and speak intimately to one another because they are strangers and what can they lose, hence the dirty phone call, and yes, yes I know this is a clean call, but I do need to know you before I can begin to make sense of what you are trying to tell me—is the hotel on fire, in Mainz?—Car? Mel? Ita? Carmelita. Well, I thank you, I have now got it, and it is not Trocadero, as I kept imagining. And your second name, your family name? Smith? Is that possible. Millions and millions of people named Smith without protest. Young lady, you must change your name to Escamillio, Armadillo Escamillio is much more correct for you than Mary Smith, or Miss or Mrs. Or Mzzzz Smith, that Mzzzz part I have never learned to pronounce I am afraid, I don't believe it can both be pronounced correctly and heard accurately, it always sounds like something in between speech. You were saying something about dinner or something or something with somebody or somebody, did I hear that part correct? In a matter of two hours? Ah, really, I'd love to, I'd love to, but no I cannot meet you in the lobby in two hours to go to dinner with you and Mr. and Mrs. Rye—not Rye, *her* name is Rye, it's her maiden name, his is Hiss, like Alger Hiss? Well, spell it then, I'm deaf, let's say no more about it? L, yes, L like lunatic? I, I, like in me, myself and I, as we used to say when we were fighting ferociously for identity. S, S like in Saint Francis or San Francisco. And finally the key letter, the animator, H, did you say? H like in home, home on the range, is it true that Franklin Delano Roosevelt used to sing that song to his mother as a growing boy? H like in heart, heart, making the name L, I, S, H, Lish. In San Francisco in 1929 there used to be a famous radio program called Blue Monday Jamboree, and one of the best of a dozen comic characters was called Tizzie Lish, but what Tizzie stands for I don't know. Miss Escamillio, please make allowances for all this talk from me but I am continuing to sleep although I am actually on the telephone speaking to you, in answer to two or three dozen rings, I really didn't want to believe the phone itself was ringing, I wanted to believe it was only a memory of phone ringings of the past, in sleep, and all of this is myself, real, in this room, in the Roemerwall Hotel in Mainz instead of in the Hilton or the Inter Continental or the Holiday Inn or one of the other international hotels of high quality and magnificent service in Frankfurter—by God, it seems to me that when weary travelers die they will get a good room in a good hotel in Frankfurt, after all. I mean, I am a willing traveler but after traveling eight or nine thousand miles I find that I want to lie down and sleep and not think of anybody or the courtesies of hearing nearby people at a table for instance and replying to what they have said, and not forgetting now and then to smile and carry on fit to kill—you are the Frankfurt representative of Usica, you say, or for short, International Communications Agency— sounds fishy—but yes, yes, I am traveling on behalf of the Agency. Even so, Usica is "sick," and the rest of the name is like a concoction in a mediocre English spy story, is there no way that our people in Washington can hustle up various writers and professors and jazz musicians to go to socialist countries to let the people see how broad we are in the variety of people we permit to breathe without let or hindrance under a more casual name, like Americans One and All? Well, yes yes, I'd love to meet such a famous writer and her husband, but not at dinner in Mainz somewhere in two hours, I am struggling to remain in dreamland with body and soul still neatly fastened together, and I know that if I force myself to keep such a dinner engagement I would have to be rotten rotten company, and it is bad enough when I am refreshed by the enormous portion of proper rest and sleep I need every now and then—I really imagined that somebody from Usica would have met me at the airport and helped me get to this dreary hotel room in Mainz, you know—where were you when I needed you? Perhaps you were all on the telephone talking to one another, is that possible?

SCENE 2

LISH

Now, in sharing the cost of this taxi ride from Mainz to the Frankfurt Airport, you paid half or forty marks, so be sure to present that sum to Washington and they will reimburse you.

MOUSTACHE

Yes, thank you. Forty marks it is, then. What is that? About five dollars, or what? I mean, I am forgetful and I have an idea I will forget this, and so I will lose five dollars. Forty marks, is that five dollars, or what?

MS RYE

Perhaps it is more. Might it be more, Daniel?

LISH

Well, let me see, I'm not sure, it can be figured out of course, but the taxi cost on the meter was eighty marks and you gave me forty, so whatever forty exchanges to, that is what the government owes you. Six dollars, maybe.

MOUSTACHE

I'll jot it down somewhere.

MS RYE

And all such expenses are to be reimbursed, are they not, Daniel?

LISH

Yes, I was told to keep a record.

MOUSTACHE

After we get tickets and luggage checked and settled may I suggest we find a coffee bar, perhaps? And you both are at Princeton, is that right? I once had a play produced at the Theatre at Princeton, but I've forgotten its name. I went from Manhattan by train and saw the play, but I didn't like the way the professors and their students had done it, although it wasn't altogether silly. And in any case after the performance the movie director George Stevens introduced himself to me and we went out to a kind of garden and sat on a bench and talked about the theatre, although actually what we really talked about was death. I hope this does not surprise you. I mean almost everything all of us ever talk about turns out to be about death, as a matter of fact, and the famous and rich director wanted to know if Jim Dandy, the fat man in the play, had some kind of symbolic meaning, and of course I laughed because I hear such ideas in conversations always with a kind of surprise that is awkward— here, here, let me take your bags, this man will let us avoid standing in the long line forever, not because we are Americans or VIPs or anything like that, he seems to want to clear us so we can go for coffee, and the people in the long line are not outraged, they are sometimes, especially in London, a city I love profoundly, partly because people who stand in long lines become outraged when somebody tries to belittle their docile acceptance of silly reality—yes, sir, Warsaw. We're going to Warsaw and I believe the flight is in about an hour, is that right? And thanks for clearing us this way.

MS RYE

Perhaps it is because we are travelers rather than Americans and don't speak German.

MOUSTACHE

But I speak fluent German.

MS RYE

You spoke English to the man.

MOUSTACHE

Only to please him, to let his English be heard by the people in the long line who at best speak English very poorly. It is a small courtesy.

MS RYE

Daniel, is it all right if I pass up the coffee? I believe I would like to visit that kiosk where I see rows of books.

LISH

I don't believe I really want coffee so soon after breakfast. I'll join you.

MOUSTACHE

The fact is I don't really want any coffee, either. I had tea at breakfast, a whole big pot, and then another, because when I first visited Russia in 1935 and there was no coffee at all, I learned to like tea first thing in the day—as if tea hadn't been the way we had always started the day in Fresno almost seventy years ago. The Germans used to translate and publish quite a few of my books, but lately they have discovered many excellent new American writers, and I am glad that they have. Harold Robbins is a very big seller in Germany, I believe.

MS RYE

How did you happen to learn to speak German?

MOUSTACHE

Well, actually, there really is no how to such things, is there? I mean, we have all dreamed of singing flawlessly in grand opera, and of playing the piano as if we might be Frederic Chopin himself, improvising for Madame George Sand, by the hour, as it were, and so all of a sudden there I was answering George Stevens in German about the meaning of the fat man in the famine. Jim Dandy. No, I said, no, Jim Dandy is only Jim Dandy.

MS RYE

I mean how did you say it in German?

MOUSTACHE

Nein, nein, Jim Dandy ist Jim Dandy—but of course the saying of the name Jim Dandy in German is slightly different than in English. Shim Tdanty is more like it is.

MS RYE
Oh?

SCENE 3

DEVIL

(Steps out of the shadows) Shall we pause a moment to consider what is going on here, folks? You and I have a common interest in this man, I believe, for we both want to take his soul, as the saying goes. Many of you have said the prayer in early childhood, and said it in good faith, sometimes totally indifferent to its awful implications and sometimes terrified of them. Now I lay me down to sleep. I pray the Lord my soul to keep. If I should die before I wake, I pray the Lord my soul to take. Well, I suppose I myself was never asked to make that prayer, although I am sure that being who I am I must have been asked to make something like a prayer of the same sort, only not quite so cheerful, if I may put it that way. What we have here is this boy, you see, traveling, and we wonder why, for he is also seventy-two years old, also that is not to confuse the matter of his identity or character, for that cannot be done, he is still this boy, perhaps we might say, Our Boy, and I want to grab him away from the Lord and make him totally one of us, a disgrace to the human race, which is really the only thing for an honorable man or woman to be, and so far one is tempted to suspect that this boy is not a disgrace, or if a disgrace, only a small disgrace and not worth noticing seriously, as the saying is. Who does he think he is to go around the world still a boy, still stupid as a boy is, still atrociously ill-mannered instead of murderously polite as the human race swiftly learns how to be in order to avoid being stopped in its tracks right where it runs. He is still a damned fool, and he doesn't even suspect as much. If the truth is told, he sometimes believes he is not only corrupt, like everybody else, like myself, and yourselves, you the people out there in literary land, theatre land, fantasy land, audience land, circus land, society land, radio land, television land,

newspaper land, and so on and so forth, why should I give
myself a headache naming the various lands in which we dwell,
or believe we do? He talks to anybody who happens to be within
hearing range, and frequently enough when he believes he is
talking to somebody he was talking to a moment ago he suddenly
notices that no, this is somebody else, somebody who may not
even understand English, but he goes right on talking, for if
the truth is told he really isn't talking to anybody in particular,
he is either talking to himself or to God, or to my own Emperor,
you know—hell fire, I'm just one of the millions of picayune
little agents who are always out on stupid assignments, as I am
out on this stupid assignment. Follow that man, hear him, if
he notices you, if he speaks to you, speak back, keep track of
where he goes and what he does, he's dying, he knows it, he
doesn't believe it, he seems to believe that death is not death,
it is more of the same, life, which he also seems to believe is
not life, although it is all the human race has, and all he also
has. So far he has been clearly rather tired, apparently near
exhaustion, and he hears telephone bells when none are ringing,
and when one telephone bell actually rings he answers it and
talks to somebody who apparently is actually at the other end
of the line, if we are willing to believe in telephones, and frankly
although we are I sometimes wonder—aren't they indeed
elements of the fantasy that has taken over the dimensions of
reality. But when he spoke to somebody who must surely have
been his daughter, that was sleep, exhausted sleep at that, and
so it was when he spoke to somebody who must surely have
been his son—both of these people out of his seed, as the saying
goes, and out of the womb of the woman who received his seed
out of total ignorance of the real consequences although there
was never any anxiety about male seed meeting female egg or
ovum or whatever it is, and it was clearly a joyousness to him
when the girl swelled and when the son was delivered of her,
and a few years later again when the girl was manufactured
in the same traditional manner and was delivered in the same
manner. They were, he has frequently said to himself, wonder
kids of the human race, they were indeed at last his own human

race, and coming of his seed, never mind whose ovum had worked with the seed, this human race was superior—and that was when I nearly had him, for when a man is that stupid about himself and his answers to all of the questions and his expectations of the future and his jubilant theories about his past, especially the unknown and unknowable past of his thousands of ancestors, oh, that is when my job is amusing, and when I know it is going to be no struggle at all for me to rope in another half-wit father—yes, mark that word: father. Mothers are different, good God how different they are, they can rape their sons and daughters alike and never know it at all. But only fathers are arrogant about the new human race they are propagating, poor bastards. Look at him go.

MOUSTACHE

Well, let's tell the story, shall we folks, this is now room 318 at the Hotel Europejski in Warsaw, and the time is 5:15 of the same day, the day that began in Mainz. It doesn't take long to get from anywhere to anywhere, and this does not mean anything else. It only means that if you go on board an airplane chances are now very good that you will soon reach another place, sometimes thousands of miles away and all you will have noticed is that you were served a kind of big meal or small meal or snack or Continental breakfast depending upon the amount of time to be used up during the flight—but look here, look here, you're standing back there by the door to the bath, what is it, old buddy boy?

DEVIL

(Now as doctor in white robe) Well, if you say so, I suppose it is so, but at the moment you are alone, and I must tell you that anything you say will not be used against you, so if you believe it might do you some kind of good to curse me, or any doctor at all, or the whole medical profession, or science itself, or measurable information, or whatever you want to call it, please feel free to do so, for we have also learned that the sighs

and groans of people serve an excellent purpose, makes them feel a little less captured, as it were.

MOUSTACHE

Oh ho, so now you're the doctor in Fresno, are you, the shy silent intelligent Armenian born in Alexandria, oh I suppose 40 years or so ago, are you? Well, that's fine, that's fine, and it isn't that I have any real quarrel with you, or with medicine men, witch doctors, voodoo boys, or with theories of therapy, theories of health, of disease, of life, of non-life, of super-life, but once again I have got to say what I said when you told me it would appear that I have cancer—of the prostate. I don't think so, Doc, because I always refer to any Doctor as Doc, and you said nothing, so I knew you believed your finger diagnosis was correct and my natural repudiation of it was incorrect. And so I told myself instantly, Christ, now I've got cancer. I mean everything is swift, everything is instantly true or untrue, everything happens in the instant: the start of life, the stop of life, and everything starting and stopping in between. What I want to say, though, is that notwithstanding Medicare and Blue Cross and insurance and anything else, doctors and nurses and hospitals cost too much. I told you once, I'll tell you again, You young doctors all over the country want to become millionaires in ten years.

DOCTOR/DEVIL

Five.

MOUSTACHE

That's right, and I rather admire your honesty, so with me it's myself tagged but with you it's another source of good big easy money, and while I can't say I begrudge you the million surely almost already stashed in the bank or in an orange grove up above Lake Wahtoke somewhere or in house and garden, in mansion with pool and gardener where the rich people live, I live where the poor people live, you know, while I really am delighted that you are doing well I don't like the diagnosis which already is established—one second after its declaration—and has already killed me, if you won't mind the silly word. Doc, my reply is this: in your language, yes, I have cancer, in my language, it is myself that I have, another variation of myself. Every man is born of his tribe, accident, and mystery, and dies of himself, but again the word dies is theoretic, we put it that way because if we didn't we might not be able to communicate by speech at all—and wouldn't that be the day. All in total silence, by means of eye and a few other things—posture, movement, gesture, scent, sigh, silence, silence, all informing us of the unstated truth. Well, it's all right, Doc, but right now I have got to receive my interpreter, everybody gets an interpreter in Warsaw, and I got the best of the lot, Martha Mularuk, who is on her way here to get me to the American Ambassador's big cocktail party for me, for Ms. Rye, for Mr. Lish, for forty-four American people of the theatre, for their counterparts of Poland, of Warsaw, and so right now I have got to get into my dark suit and you've got to get back into your own realm, am I right, as we say? So I've got cancer, so what? I've got it in the prostate, so what? Didn't the sweet Mexican lady who mopped the floor of my private room at the Sierra Hospital say, Oh, that's nothing. My father had it, he died of something else? And didn't our old pal Doc Leo himself say, Well, if you've got to have cancer, that's a good place to have it? I mean, what's the big deal? *(Knock)* Come in, come in.

MARTHA
I thought you were on the phone, who were you talking to?

MOUSTACHE
Myself. God. I was trying out some lines for a play.

SCENE 4

MOUSTACHE

Cocktail party. In Warsaw. At the American Embassy itself, and across the street is the Embassy of the People's Republic of Mongolia, and I wish to Christ I were there, not here. Actually this may not be the embassy itself, it may be the home of the Ambassador, and he is a damned nice man, let's get that straight at the outset, for such matters are important, are they not? I should say so. I have his name some place but it's not in my head, or memory, it's on the card the pretty interpreter passed along to me when we went down to the lobby of the Europejski (I can't pronounce Polish spelling of words, that's all, and right now Poles are in the American government and in the Roman Catholic Church, as we all know).

ALAN, PRODUCER-DIRECTOR

Bill, you never get old, do you? Remember me? Alan Shoulder, we met in New York thirty years ago, and then twenty years ago, and once it was at the poor rich boy's who had to be in the theatre, and you told him to go ahead and produce *Waiting for Godot*, and he hired me to stage it, and I did, and it won all the prizes. Alan Shoulder?

MOUSTACHE

Schneider, why do you keep saying Shoulder?

ALAN

You keep hearing Shoulder—is your shoulder broken? I keep saying Schneider, you keep hearing shoulder. What is it?

MOUSTACHE

It's the acoustics, you don't get acoustics at cocktail parties in Warsaw the way you used to get acoustics. Of course I remember you, man, you are one of the best all-around directors of plays in America. Michael Myerberg said, What about this play *Waiting for Godot*, and I said, Produce it, lose some of your money, it's a great play, but do you know I never knew until this minute that you directed it, although I was glad to hear that Bert Lahr played Estragon or the other bum, I never got them straight, and I don't suppose Samuel Beckett ever did either. One was nearly the same as the other. Now, if there were more than five or six people in the play, counting the small boy, and they were all the same, that would be fun. What are you doing in Poland? You haven't moved back, have you? I mean, Darryl Zanuck used to kid around about some of his hired help, his stooges, and one of his favorite expressions was, I wish he'd go back to Poland. I suppose Darryl Zanuck's grandfather or somebody came from Poland, do you suppose? I mean, what are you doing here at this cocktail, as we say in Paris. This is a command appearance for me, as we say, and I arrived only a short time ago from Frankfurt—did you ever get a room at a hotel in Frankfurt—I have never met a human being who has, although when I went to the Book Fair a couple of years ago I was told that an American writer had a suite not just a room at one of the bigger and newer and better hotels but I can't remember if it was Alex Haley or Alex Vonnegut or Alex Buchwald. I was told to be here, so I'm here.

ALAN

So was I. Who told you?

MOUSTACHE

Martha Mularuk told me, that's who, and I'm sure you must know who she is. My own private interpreter. Who told you?

ALAN

Somebody like that, but let me tell you something—again, I mean, you never change, you don't grow old, you'll live to be a hundred. I'm old, I'm tired, and I look it, don't I?

MOUSTACHE

You look the same as ever, as I remember it, but who are all these intense screaming people all around?

ALAN

Oh, they're theatre people, mostly from non-commercial, from schools, from little non-profit places that get funded from the big new Santa Claus in Washington.

MOUSTACHE

Is that you speaking that way, or is that me thinking that way. I mean, you've been funded by the government for twenty years or more yourself, haven't you? Did John Kennedy start all that, and if he did should we be enchanted or should we feel the way I do. They should have all taken jobs at the supermarkets, there is more real theatre at the checkout stand than in any of their theatres. How much money did Mike Myerberg lose on *Waiting for Godot?* Twenty thousand dollars?

ALAN

Lose? He made money. And I'm suing the estate; they still haven't paid me or given me a small percentage, the rats.

MOUSTACHE

We call them ratons, it's Spanish, means rats.

ALAN

By God, you'll live to be a hundred.

MOUSTACHE

Either I already have, and maybe twice over, or you are mistaken. I'm tagged, I'm performing robust health, and it is very wearing to do that. Give me an audience, even of one, with two dozen hanging around listening, like right here, and I've got to perform, I don't know why. You'd think I had a mission in the world, wouldn't you. Well, maybe I do, maybe I do, maybe it's true.

SAROYAN

Now, ladies and gentlemen, by your leave, and all that stuff, the writer himself comes out of the woodwork and enters into the play and perhaps even into the spirit of it, for as we know anything is possible if anybody says so, and everybody these days is saying so, from little infants just beginning to put four or five words together into sentences of protest, as a rule, although now and then the beautiful little creatures, or should we say monsters, lapse into poetry, of sorts. And so now I say I am the writer, I am not any of the others so far in this play, I am the writer of it, by name Saroyan, first name William, not Aram, or Petros as the name might have been after the father's father instead of William after the father's friend who went to a Protestant Heaven a few months before I came into a Protestant or non-denominational Reality—rather than Hell, Earth, Life, Place, Confusion, Confabulation, or Theory, to name only a few of the words and meanings which might be easily placed upon where we are once we are born and have not yet died. But why have I come out of the shadows into the glare of the lights or even the sharper or sharpest glare of the spotlight in this manner? What do I mean by it? And how is this to serve you, the people, about whom all of the concern of everything and everybody, all science, reason, and art has gathered like bees about the Queen in the hive—ugly, really, you know, as so much of nature is, and one of the reasons for art in the first place, most likely? I have done this, this coming out of the woodwork and shadows because frankly it has seemed to me something right to do, although I expect this rightness soon enough to settle down into the traditional wrongness of pretty much everything we do—we, mind you, not nature, for while we are stuck to nature helplessly we also have always been compelled to believe we are free of it, we are not like the animals, the plants, and the inert rocks, and all the rest of it: we are man, man himself, male and female, each in place, each habitually stuck together for continuance in the very manner of the animals, in the continuation of nature's force and truth, and we do things nature is unable to do, never mind that nature has no reason to reason, no need to laugh, no wish to manufacture balances and proportions and rhythms, for it has them all and has always had them—but there is the traveler in this play, the old man in the old body, with the sad old face and the enormous old white moustache, and is he not myself, is he not Saroyan of the tribe which lived for centuries in the Highlands of Armenia, at the city of Baghesh, later called Bitlis? Well, of course he is, but he damned well isn't, too, and if the truth is told, and here comes the fun, I myself right here right now at this very moment am not he who I say I am, I am not the actual man named Saroyan, I am either an actor performing a part in a play, this play, or even if I myself, that is William Saroyan himself happens to do this part, and it isn't very likely in this world or the next, I would still not be William Saroyan of the rest of the Truth, so to put it, I would be a performance, and the fun quickens when we understand that even in the rest of the Truth, in the Truth of world and reality themselves I am a performer and always have been, and so have you, dear soul, whoever you are, man or woman, boy or girl, we have no choice, and if we don't seem to be acting and seem to be acted upon that also is acting, if you can follow, and I am sure you can, although I am not willing to believe that you should. That matter of what any of us ought to choose to do or think, and how or when and so on, is the good big matter of our way and probable truth, but one thing at a time, please, I say to myself. We are all fast asleep, you know, at this meeting, in this play, whether it is being performed or read or even ignored, we are all of us always part of a continuation of ancient human sleep, distinguished from the sleep of sheep, in that we the people remember however indistinctly everything we experience in sleep, century after century, and here we are doing a very very small amount of it in the English language, which is at best relatively a new one and only occasionally the means to something like a satisfactory summing up of all of the stuff that arrives so abundantly and swiftly that only summing up is a slight possibility, and even then for only an instant of the charge of it all upon us as we meander to the end of the road, as I am meandering at this very moment, both in the play and in the body, in mind and memory—Lord, I am near the end of my 72nd year, to what do I owe this incredible distinction, and how shall I use it most effectively? Is it by the writing of this play and the entering into it in person as it were? Yes, that would appear to be so, and I thank you.

MOUSTACHE

So now we have met himself, the playwright, and as the saying goes we have seen everything. It just isn't done, but it has been done, so on with the dance. Here is this little girl at the Fresno Court House Park Sunday night concert dancing up front because the music won't permit her to stand still. Well, she is a fish in sweet water, but what happened to her, whatever happened to her we don't know. Fade fade fade fade, fade out O shade of truth, in the rockpool are little fish and ferns and water-skaters and the two eyes of each of us studying the language of that perfection and silence. Here now we are at the University of Warsaw, three of us from places in America, answering the questions of students of the English language. May I ask, ladies and gentlemen, young women and young men, boys and girls, how many of you are writers, kindly raise your hands. Not one hand, so I presume every one of you is a writer but a shy writer, and I congratulate you on your shyness, it is better to be shy at the beginning of a career than at the end, for that, as you see, is the time for pride and noise. You, then, ask your question, and one or another of us here will see to the answering of it.

WOMAN

I would like to ask Elena Rye, At the beginning of your career did you find opposition to it—from your family, for instance, or from your teachers, or from your friends, or from society at large?

MS RYE

That is a very complicated question, isn't it? I wonder if I can begin to answer even a little of it, because you see...

MAN

We can't hear you, could you speak up just a little, perhaps?

MS RYE

I was asked if anybody didn't believe I ought to write, and I
began to say I don't quite know how to answer the question,
because in my . . .

WOMAN

We still can't hear you, we who are here at the back of the hall.

MS RYE

Because in my family there was always an atmosphere of rather
pleasant enthusiasm about whatever any of us imagined we might
like to do. I hope you can hear me, but if you can't I'm afraid
we must imagine that the loudspeakers are not working properly.
Is that possible? No, I don't believe I was ever aware of any
hostility from anybody about my writing. Of course I tried to
keep the matter to myself, for at the very beginning I myself
wanted to know if I could indeed take my ambition seriously,
and the only way I could find out was to write and then carefully
consider what I had written. I found that from the very beginning
it was always a kind of unaccountable baroque or highly
ornamental order of writing which in turn carried me rather
helplessly into areas of human experience that surprised even
me—terrible malevolence among unexpected people, ravenous
appetites, horrible crimes, betrayals, conspiracies of the most
terrible kind, and there I was, writing it all, there I was the
author of it all. I hope I haven't made a reply that is useless
to the person who asked the question and confusing to some
of the rest of you. I suspect, from the question, that the asker
has experienced opposition from one or two quarters, possibly
society at large, or even the state, if I may put it that way.

MAN

I would like to ask Mr. Buddington, When you write a poem
do you know what you want to say?

WARSAW VISITOR

BUDDINGTON

Well, it just so happens that I have in this book a poem that rather neatly answers that question—if I can find it.

MOUSTACHE

While Mr. Buddington is turning pages back and forth looking for the poem that answers the question, perhaps I can mention that Carl Sandburg at his home in Harbert, Michigan on the Lake asked me to go with him to a cocktail party at a neighbor's house, and when we got there he opened his last book of poems, *The People, Yes,* and began to read, or chant, the first seven or eight lines. The seventy or eighty people in the room stopped their happy drinking and chatting with one another to listen to the poet, for they expected him to read for no longer than half a minute, but after two full hours he stopped reading because he had read every line in the whole book, the room was empty, except for me. Have you found the poem, Mr. Buddington?

BUDDINGTON

Well, I've forgotten the question, and the poem I thought I was looking for. What was it that I was asked?

MAN

When you write a poem do you know what you're doing?

BUDDINGTON

Well, I suppose so, I mean if a poet thinks it is time to write a poem, he thinks he knows that he wants to write a poem.

WOMAN

Why did Carl Sandburg read the whole book?

MOUSTACHE

Well, I believe he was exhausted from having just finished his biography of Lincoln. Edmund Wilson wrote that the worst thing that ever happened to Lincoln was for Carl Sandburg to write his life.

SCENE 5

DEVIL

(In full regalia) Well, it's my turn again, as we see, don't we?
Something is going on here that is far less than meets the eye,
or so I once heard somebody brilliant say about one or another
of William Shakespeare's revered plays, perhaps *Measure for
Measure,* perhaps *A Midsummer Night's Dream,* perhaps
Coriolanus, what do we care about such details, our job is to
bring down the human race in total disgrace, if I may: race
and disgrace, that is: any English teacher will tell you that such
a piece of doggerel rhyme just won't do. At any rate, a story
is being told in play form, possibly even on a stage with actors,
possibly only in a book, with only one reader, about somebody
or other who has a name and something like several aliases,
so to put it. Who is he? Well, we could certainly say, Sir, he
is yourself. Who is Hamlet excepting each of us reading his
lines and the play in which he figures. Well, as you surely must
remember, we had no trouble with Hamlet at all, he was fair
game from the word go and easy to bring down along with just
about everybody else in his world supposedly because his mother
had gone to work and entered the bed of Hamlet's father's
brother, that poor nincompoop of a sad silly fellow. We brought
down Hamlet and the whole human race like child's play, which
of course the play itself is. A grown man carrying on like a
silly petulant child and nobody to say briskly, Stop it. Although
it was only three or four hundred years ago that Shakespeare
wrote his plays the human race has failed to produce a successor,
and it may very well be that this has been a blessing for if the
truth is told all art needs its time and culture, and for at least
a century we have got another kind of society and meaning and
connection to everything unresolved and so our art is entirely
different, isn't it. Try to think what Leonardo would have
thought of the art of Picasso. Would he not have said, Sir, I
say Sir, shame on you, and get away from me, that's all, just
get as far away from me as possible. With me, simply a poor
agent of the Big Boy, the Big Shot, so to put it, it is another

Get entirely: Get thee hence, that is to say. Satan, get thee hence. Oh, how the righteous fear being seduced in any one of its dozens of ways, but always thinking of the most obvious ways and all the way being far gone into the more complicated ways—virtue itself, boys and girls, is fraudulent, as we began to suspect from the first day of study, did we not? I say Sir, Sir, did we not?

MOUSTACHE

Jesus, can't a man lie down and rest in the afternoon of a hard day in Warsaw, in Poland, without having you take stage center front and start blathering all over the place? You're a clown, do you know?

DEVIL

Do you say a clown does not know a thing or two? Then, Sir, I say Sir right back to you, widen the range of your reading, for a careful reading of everybody's story, whether he tells it himself or his disciples tell it or the best biographers tell it, is the story of a clown. Surely you know that, and furthermore I would most likely find myself horrified if you were not willing to acknowledge that you yourself are a clown and always have been, everything you did made the human race laugh, so far as the race was near enough to observe. Deny it. You can't. And it is still going on. Before you open your big mouth to say something people are so sure it is going to be comic that they break into laughter. It happened again and again this afternoon while the other two members of the literary panel tried to restore order to the overall situation. If you want stage center, by God, it is yours, I only fill in now and then, and I must say I enjoy doing so. Shall I go back into the crowded shadows and wait or shall we chat a bit?

MOUSTACHE

I told you I'm tired, and I've got a big and busy evening straight ahead. The official dinner with the writers of Warsaw, carefully chosen of course, with lots of pouring of drinks and lots of pork—they've got no beef, I hate pork except when it is roasted by the Chinese, especially of San Francisco, and then it is no longer pork as we know it, it is something created the way art is. And of course I shall strain and strain to hear first what the boys and girls are saying in Polish and then when Martha Mularuk—don't I find that name irresistible, though?—puts it all into English, which, although rather correct, to me either sounds like Polish also or like something said in a language entirely beyond the range of philology. Talk away, clown, I have got to rest some more, I don't want to chat at all.

DEVIL

Well, I was only saying, Here in Warsaw we have this old fool of an American writer, by way of Armenia, the highland city of Bitlis, and if the truth is told so far he is performing as if he were himself in 1935 when he first arrived back in Europe and crossed Poland and spent a night in Lvov or Lemberg. What's eating the boy? Why does he want to perform at all?

MOUSTACHE

The days of travel are easy days but they are hard days, too. They are much harder, almost, than the days of full leisure, when a man can choose how he is to take up one minute to the next for twenty-four hours, and suddenly discovers that so much absence of tension is a source of much tension of another order. So what do you do, what do you do? Well, what I did was go where the program told me to go and I must say the work of it was easy, it was fun, it was nothing, and it was for a good cause. Literature. By God, I enjoy saying that. Think of it. Literature. Here I am a published writer for nearly half a century and everywhere I go my name is known, if my writing isn't, although mainly it is. That is a very large if tiny thing, don't you think? It certainly amuses me to try to guess what I seem to the various people of Warsaw I have met so far as well as the people on the program fetched here by Usica, as I have said: a sick running together of first letters of five words which mean simply United States International Communication

85

Agency—hoo boy, it's fun, is it not. Usica. No, you don't sica, boys and girls, ladies and gentlemen, all you do is go from place to place and drink and eat and talk and try to hear what the main people are saying—in the form of questions directed to you. This is a favorite, because Poland is a socialist country: what is the responsibility of the writer? And then the question goes on sometimes to society, mankind, history, but best of all to the matter of the prevention of the neutron war, so to put it, the suicidal war, the criminal war, the stupid war, and all the rest of it. And if ever there was a question suitable for an answer by anybody under the age of eight that is it. But one learns to be very thoughtful and courteous about the foolish questions and the good boys and girls who ask them: party members, and by boys not one of them may be understood to be under forty-four at least, and by girls not one of them may be understood to be under let's say thirty-two and let it go at that, but they are members of the Party and very watchful of one another, and yet also very warm and friendly, for I certainly have never felt from any of them anything less than kindly thoughtfulness—everything for my comfort, but little do they know or suspect that there can be nothing from them for my comfort, it has got to come from myself or be damned. And such kindly thoughtfulness from myself is becoming very rare these days, it would seem. Which is one of the better reasons I am on this foray, this assignment, this journey, this piece of science, this tour of duty as it were of a very unlikely patriot, working on behalf of his government (which is bloody with crime and ruthlessness of spirit toward even its very own people, never mind other people, on behalf of the feeble but persistent expectation of restoring the American at large to an image of at least a decent tolerableness, to exempt him from the appearance of ugliness and the reality of being insufferable, on behalf of presenting to a few people of the arts, especially of literature, an American who if nothing else is at least guileless and incapable of conspiracy, a man who laughs at the tradition of spies working the world and sending in their stupid reports, on behalf of easy-going dismissal of homage, even if deserved, by peers and colleagues, and pretty much on behalf of the inevitable surprise of an American who really appears to be no such thing, although he also does not appear to be especially European either). Only a few hours ago we visited the famous Park of Warsaw where I was absolutely fascinated by two statues: one rather modern of Frederic Chopin where free concerts are given every Sunday to people at large including tourists, and always with a very good pianist performing, whether man or woman, and the other down the slope steadily three hundred yards or so to a kind of al fresco place beside an artificial lake where a half dozen pieces of apparently ancient sculpture are to be seen, and one of these pieces really took hold of my soul: for it was the woman I always wanted to find and never did, reclining somewhere with a cherub of some sort hovering very near, her neck and head and face incredibly right and irresistible. Now of course the sculpture is very probably famous and by one of the greatest boys of world sculpture, but who am I to know who he is or who she is, although I suspect each is famous, super famous. Afterwards walking where the swans swim or settle upon the walks themselves, unafraid of people passing at sundown, we were taken by car to The Actors Club where a dozen writers welcomed three or four of us who had come from America: and we ate roast duck and it was good if just a little heavy. For literature.

A man lives his life, does his work, performs his function of maintaining continuance—of what? Of self, a fantasy: of family, a kind of modest statistical or factual reality: of the human race, such as it is, a very sound actuality: in short, he begins, as the Old Testament puts it, and never mentions through whom he did so, as if it was irrelevant who the female was, and of course that's silly, as Hebrew law long ago established: never mind who the father is, if the mother is Hebrew the child is Hebrew. A man avoids death by accident or from boredom every day and suddenly notices that he is by cracky, as we say, thirty years old. That old, really? I expected to die before the age of twenty-four. And then he notices that he is forty. Then fifty, half a century. Isn't that enough? And then sixty. And still he goes on and I'll tell you why. He doesn't know any better. He hasn't come anywhere near knowing any better. He runs like a schoolboy not to be late for the bell, to avoid embarrassment, humiliation, ridicule, disgrace, mockery, and if you like death itself. And on and on this goes and the man is suddenly seventy and he can't understand what to make of it for he feels precisely as he felt when he was seven, for instance, or seventeen or twenty-seven. What a book is the book of the world, that's all I can say, both as a reader and as a writer. What a magnificent book it is and how little, how terribly little it tells us about ourselves or indeed about anything at all although it seems to tell us everything, especially since the discovery a few years ago of the printing press. Why has the telling been so poor? Because there hasn't been anything to tell. Language was a giving over to a longing to stop, to rest. It was a substitute for the act, and the business of the living, of any order, is to act. Writing about acting is rather handsome in a way but it is essentially confusing at best. At first it was talk of course, and somebody found out how to make marks and signs that could approximate in a comparatively permanent form the meaning of the talk. Ah, well, this is silly, this is beside the point, I ate the roast duck with the writers at The Actors Club on an unknown and even mysterious street in Warsaw and the writer to my left asked many questions, a man who had once visited New York, and the writer to my right asked many questions, a woman who received the Lenin Prize for something or other— was it Peace?—a few years ago, and I have such rotten hearing, as I told each of them again and again, and yet they continued to speak as if anything they said was heard by me as clearly as it was known to them in their own heads—and the strain of all this listening gave me something like esophagitis, as I believe it is called—a stoppage of the ability to swallow—but I prayed devoutly and stopped trying to know what they were saying and asked God and Heaven and Nature to kindly take away the bubble like the stone at the cave and let me swallow so that I would not have to leave the table and go either to the can or to the street and throw up the bubble and quietly make my way back to my place as if nothing had happened, and sure enough my prayer was answered, and I rejoiced. By God, sometimes this condition does not disappear even after throwing up not once but three or four times, and then hiccuping all over the place and waiting and sweating and asking God to lay off, please—I am a young man, don't embarrass me, please. And so I resumed sipping the red wine and chewing and swallowing the roast duck, and I got through the dinner rather neatly, if I say so myself, all things considered. The place was noisy being a club for actors, a noisy people, so that I was not able to hear anything from any other part of the table, although I seemed to notice that the other delegates from America, the other writers, seemed to be having the same kind of time, and dinner, as I was having, except without the esophagitis or whatever it is, and the praying, and the gratitude of having the prayer answered. Such a thing is virtually a miracle, but unsung, unnoticed, and if brought to the attention of Rome would surely be ridiculed.

This is a play, and I am one of the players in the play, if not indeed the main player, for the play is about this American writer who in his 72nd year finishes a big new book in Fresno and instantly informs Usica by letter that now, having done his work, he was ready to hear about any program brought up several months ago, and so one thing led to another, it was all worked out, and the man began to go and go and arrive and arrive and now days later, months later, years later, here I am an actor playing the part of this man, or here you are reading about it all in a book, reading the play itself, as published by somebody or other somewhere along the line.

But I also am this man himself, standing and writing at his fifth floor flat in Paris, now a week since he flew out of the fifth country on his itinerary, from Belgrade to Paris, and began to occupy the dusty flat again, as he had once a year for twenty years. This is me, an actor, but it is also him, the man himself, the real article, the McCoy, the writer born in Fresno, eight or nine thousand miles from Bitlis, in 1908, the rebel, the refuser, the friend of everybody, the critic and enemy of everybody also, fraudulence is tolerable if it is amusing, but it is an outrage to the soul if it is criminal, if it kills, and lies kill, deception kills, and all, all, all of these things, which are one thing, drive me up a wall, for I am helplessly stupid and righteous. I know that the world itself, the human race itself is a lie and that treachery is natural, but it drives me up a wall just the same. How am I to stay alive and have it mean a little something or other in a world and among people which and who are false? Well, however it may be, I have somehow managed, haven't I? I mean I'm still here, although now suddenly in Warsaw for the first time in all my years. It's so isn't it?

DEVIL

You know, I've been standing back there in the shadows listening to you and woolgathering at the same time and I'll be damned if I know what you have been saying or what you are saying now. Is it possible that talk, that writing itself, in the end must be noticed to have said nothing at all? I mean, what the hell are you saying? What is all this fanfarola, man?

MOUSTACHE

Fanfarola, man? Where did you get fanfarola from, pray tell? Well, I'll tell you, Red Tail, I'll tell you exactly what this is all about. Nothing, nothing, by God nothing at all. It is only the lonely ravings of a stupid madman, because he is tagged, because it is time, now, as we heard in the famous Pub in Dublin in 1939, Time, gentlemen, time, and Flann O'Brien and I and four or five others accepted the rules and drove to Jim Whelan's at Stepaside and continued to drink and shout and carouse, as the word has it. Man, it is time. It is time. And who can understand such a truth, and doesn't the poor fellow find it impossible not to believe that perhaps even though it is time that it is not time? How about that?

ACT ONE/SCENE 5

DEVIL

Yes, how about it, it doesn't make sense at all, does it, but there is one thing I want you to know because I consider it very courteous of you: I mean your refusal to give over, because as long as you are in there fighting then of course my little assignment has an element of drama in it and I can go on expecting the unexpected. You refuse to give over, to lie down and die, and I thank you for that.

MOUSTACHE

Don't thank me, it is nothing of my own doing, I know nothing about it, how does a man lie down and die? I have read the accounts of the deaths of all sorts of people, necessarily they were famous people for nobody cares how the rest of the people die, although it is surely precisely the same, and I have never got the hang of what it is that actually happens, although in the end somebody comes from the bedside out of a room and announces in a stupid hushed voice, It is over. Well, God Almighty, it was over long long ago, but damned if I am going to keep moving back and back there and then in that first breath. You are tagging along because somewhere or other some of us allowed ourselves to believe that every man's end, his death, is the consequence of devilish desire to humiliate health, solid flesh, flawless function, a man's illusion that he is alive and is never going to die. Well, have your fun, old boy with the Red Tail, but I'm away ahead of you and I am beyond being belittled by the inevitable. Of course I shall die whether you are hovering in the shadows or faded back into the focus of false reality. You are myself, and if I am not thyself, so to put it, it comes to the same thing. All this talk, this mumbling, this ruminating, is the silly but perhaps sophisticated ravings of a fighter of fraudulence, a writer of kindergarten simplicity, a lover of the pathetic human race, a hater of the treachery born into that race, and himself altogether the same as the entire race in structure and contradiction and the same as any member of it at the guillotine block for unspeakable crimes, at the hangman's platform for the destruction of New York City itself,

91

strapped in the Electric Chair for deliberately pressing the Horrible Button that sent the machinery of Neutron Bombs into action all around the world. Shall I cry out I didn't do it? just because I didn't do it? Then who in God's name did do it, since I am a writer, and have put the very writing on the wall itself, telling of it? That's what all this mumbling is about, boy.

DEVIL

There was always a game, wasn't there, between you know who and you know who, am I right?

MOUSTACHE

Yes, you are right, yes, you are not right, no, you are wrong, no, you are not wrong, there was never a game between anybody and anybody, but go ahead, let's have it, what is the game, as you understand it?

DEVIL

Well, I can only say I don't rightly know what the game is, because that is the truth, and if you think I am any less concerned about the truth than you are, or anybody else is, perhaps we have misunderstood one another. Still, still, still, as they say, leave us not argue among ourselves while the ship sinks, you know, let us be friends as we always have been or at any rate enemies as we have always been, for it is the part about always, always that permits us to be charitable about one another. If I haven't been around forever, like, I very much doubt if you would have the nostalgic and even sentimental feeling for me that you do have, am I right, and please don't mind too much my asking am I right, it is because I am really so uncertain, and if I had a mother it seems to me I would phone her for reassurance. Isn't that what all of the boys and girls are doing these days, dialing direct, I mean, the boys to speak to Mama, dear girl, and the girls to speak to Father, dear boy. Is any of this making any sense to you in Warsaw, Poland?

MOUSTACHE

Of course it's making sense. All of it is, and you are right, you are not wrong, but what is this game you are trying to summon up from some kind of legend and lore of himself and itself, or itself and himself, or noself and noself?

DEVIL

Faust, man. You've heard of Faust, I do believe. A long living German in Weimar wrote a play about Faust and himself in the form of itself, as you put it, and I believe it was made into an opera, and a glorious soprano sang somebody and a great basso sang Faust, and another sang itself, as you like to put it, and it was awfully awfully awfully—boring, don't you know.

MOUSTACHE

I heard about it. I never read Wolfgang's *Faust* and I never saw the opera, whoever composed the music, whoever wrote the libretto, but if it is so, if it all happened, so what, pray tell, so what?

DEVIL

Wolfgang? Are you sure. Isn't that the dear name of the dear little wonder child, Amadeus something or other.

MOUSTACHE

Mozart? Perhaps it is, I get the names all jumbled together, and why shouldn't I? Everybody is everybody, and sometimes the sopranos and the bassos overlap and the sweet girl grows a moustache without ever wanting to or having any biological right or reason to do so, and the basso goes swish swishing about after the performance, yes you are very probably right, Wolfgang Amadeus Mozart is his name and was his name and if you were to have met him in his day you would surely have found him insufferable for knowing, by God, knowing, knowing, knowing, by God, that he was the beloved of God himself.

DEVIL

Language, Sir, I say Sir, watch your language, surely it is not desirable or necessary to provoke the Unknown, whatever it may be, with the taking of sacred names in vain. Mozart was a darling child from everything I have ever heard about it, why do you put him down?

MOUSTACHE

I'm thinking about Goethe who lasted longer and knew a little more about what it is to be a man in a body than the boy wonder, and what I am uncertain about is his name, although I do believe it might very well have been Wolfgang, but alas, do not ask me to tell you his last words.

DEVIL

What were his last words?

MOUSTACHE

The poor old fool said, Really? Really? Really? Something like that. Or so I seem to believe I once read somewhere, but it may have been the last words of somebody else, possibly even a great grandfather in my own damned family coming to the end at the age of thirty-six or so, in Bitlis, and overheard by a great grandmother who passed along the astonishing last words. As for the Weimar boy, I don't know. He may have said nothing at the time that is set aside for the last words. He may have felt, Haven't I said my stupid last words all my life, why are you hanging about waiting for me to say something really special. What could I possibly say? Isn't it silly to expect an old fool to say something wise with his last breath? They asked Prof Kalfayan in Fresno, Prof old pal, what can we get you, and they knew he knew his goose was cooked, and the old boy said very clearly, Girls, get me girls, and died. Weren't you there?

DEVIL

Oh, I was there all right, in one way or another, but the game, what's the game?

MOUSTACHE

The game is somebody to lose and somebody to win. I lose, you win. You lose, I win. Something like that.

SAROYAN

So here a full month after Warsaw and a week after the country of the last stop on the Program, Yugoslavia, I stand in the flat in Paris I bought twenty years ago and consider how I am to live and how to die, and if you think such thinking is dismal and really silly you are right, for there is really no such thing apparently as either of the big deals, living and dying, there is only being, and this being is different, it is of itself, the human character has nothing to do with it, it is nature pure and simple, and the purpose of this intrusion is simply to remark that now apparently the cancer, the tumor of the cancer, attached to and working out of the prostate, is growing—by leaps and bounds, as I have heard it put on occasion—and this growth, this growing, this enlargement, this displacement of space, pushing upon another space and things in space is being felt, and not nicely, as we say. It is painful sitting down, getting up, standing, although once up standing is all right as it is right now as I stand at the easel beside the window upon the terrace and type, even though here in the play, whether actually being performed or being read, I am probably not typing, I am probably only standing and saying my lines. All of this is deliberate, to make known somewhat the connection of the inaccurate real with the inaccurate artful, the event in its happening and the event in its usage as something remembered and placed appropriately in a kind of vast apparently unending collage of the immaterial, of matter which has no body, which is all action and thought, so to say, and if I won't do this, if I won't try to do it, who will? Nobody I know would be so foolish, so perhaps this is all on behalf of science, art, reality, truth, history, and whatever.

Whatever, people are saying whatever to one another whenever
someone falters over a name of a person or a place,
demonstrating a failure of memory or of the capacity to invent
on the run, to lie, to deceive, and all that sort of thing, which
everybody must do now and then out of politeness if not out
of a need to avoid embarrassment, and so on and so forth. That's
all. I've come out of the shadows to make known that in the
very midst of this thing, this play, this essay at the making out
of something unknown something now known, this certain
failure, this definite mischance, there is a man of flesh and blood,
ease and disease, and I am that man, and I am making known
how it is, how it was, with me in body as I worked at the making
of this thing, because no matter what, where, when, how, or
why, it is my work to make something out of the stuff that goes
out anonymously precisely as it came in. Only with me it became
urgent to notice the coming in and thereby to render it more
universal than anonymous, and perhaps even personal, my own,
if not private, and having done that, then to notice also the going
out of it, changed as it had been, and all of this, this joyousness
of action, of combat if you will, has been to deprive death, or
meaninglessness, of its sum-total mockery of my father, of
myself, of my son, of my daughter, of you, and of yourself,
and all of that which you imagine is yours, as anybody may
easily believe a son is his son rather than the simple truth which
is that a son is his own, although with connections, such as they
are—but I was shocked that my father was effaced suddenly
not having any further continuance, or death, leaving to his heirs,
to me, six rattan-seat chairs of the kind that are popular in certain
restaurants and which I have come to cherish beyond all
furniture, if you don't mind. And a few theological books, which
are in clear English but essentially unreadable because they say
very specific things but don't really seem to be saying anything.
I did not like what happened to my father, or rather what
happened to me when my father's continuance was stopped once
and for all, and his substance, he himself was put away to rot
in the cemetery in San Jose, California only a stone's throw,
as we say, from the Southern Pacific Railroad Tracks—well,

I like that, at any rate. But I was really angry at the absurdity of the life and death of Armenak Saroyan, and I'll tell you why: he should have lived, there was no reason to die of a ruptured appendix, but there we are, he got it, and it got him, and he died, and there I was not quite three years old and altogether unable to remember what had happened and where that put me. So now, twice his age, when he was clonked dead, I have got various symptoms known to the medical profession and not exactly the best order of luck, so to say, but also not exactly the worst. I mean, I am saying in the midst of this play that I myself may go on for another full month, year, or even decade, and this play itself, this excerpt from what I knew, will be altogether, I concluded, itself, and real in itself as if I did not make it.

ACT TWO

SCENE 1

MARTHA

The curtain will go up in fifteen minutes, if you still want to go to the famous Jewish Theatre of Warsaw.

MOUSTACHE

What did you say? I mean, Ms. Rye is speaking very softly to half a dozen members of the P.E.N. Club of Warsaw?

LISH

Shhhhhhhhhhhhhhh.

MARTHA

Here, let us stand over here, away from the panel, where we will not disturb them. The play is called *Who Am I?* It was written by a German in 1929 before Adolph Hitler became who he became. It is in the form of a cabaret. Do you want to see it?

MOUSTACHE

Of course, of course. If there is a Jewish Theatre in Warsaw still, I have got to see it in action, no matter what the play happens to be.

MARTHA

Shall I inform the panel?

MOUSTACHE

Oh, no, that would be really fatheaded.

MARTHA

Well, here is our car and chauffeur. What is fatheaded?

MOUSTACHE

Well, when I use the word it usually means that somebody has misunderstood both himself and others, and there is nothing back there at the P.E.N. Club discussion that needs to be understood or misunderstood. You saw the members of the Club for yourself. They are writers, but of course not really, they almost never are really writers when they accept membership in the P.E.N. Club, or positions of high rank, like President. About thirty years ago I received a letter asking me to please accept the office of President of International P.E.N., and I didn't even answer the letter.

MARTHA

Why not? That is a very big honor, isn't it?

MOUSTACHE

Not to me, but I would never find it necessary or desirable to say that now and then such a Club as P.E.N. does not serve a good purpose.

MARTHA

You should have accepted that great honor.

MOUSTACHE

No, you are mistaken, dear pretty little girl, Martha Mularuk, for I am not an acceptor, you see, of anything fatheaded.

MARTHA

There's that word again. Why is the P.E.N. Club fatheaded?

MOUSTACHE

Because it is full of fatheads, that's why.

MARTHA

Who got the job, then? After you did not even have the courtesy to reply to the invitation?

MOUSTACHE

Well, I'm not sure, but soon enough I noticed on another letter from the Club about a campaign to rescue sixty-two thousand writers around the world in jails in every country excepting the United States that the letter was signed by the President—Miller, but not Henry Miller, for I knew his signature from some letters he had sent me in 1935 from Paris to San Francisco begging me for the love of God to rush him twenty-five dollars by telegraph or he would soon be dead. Henry is now 88 years old and living pleasantly enough in the most fashionable part of Hollywood, a territory called Pacific Palisades, where Salka Viertal, dear lady, kept open house to just about everybody who had escaped from Hitler to sunny California. And it was not Joaquin Miller, although if it had been, that dear old fraud would have been just right for the job.

MARTHA

But what about the writers in jail all over the world?

MOUSTACHE

I really don't know, I really don't know, but I am willing to believe each of them deserved to be quickly released and permitted to hurry somewhere sunny, possibly even to Pacific Palisades, although by that time Salka Viertal had sold her famous place and moved to a village in Switzerland where finally she died. That is the way it goes, you know. People going into that famous house always used to marvel that the kitchen sent forth the smell of baking strudels and fruit and spice pastries of all kinds, and Salka Viertal herself always looked like some such delicious and sweet-smelling achievement of gingerbread warmth and sympathy. What were the P.E.N. writers back there asking, did you happen to listen?

MARTHA

The interpreter told us all in very good English what they asked, and surely you heard, surely your hearing is not that bad.

MOUSTACHE

It is very bad, what did they ask?

MARTHA

Well, the big question was, What is the responsibility of the contemporary world to the writer?

MOUSTACHE

What?

MARTHA

Oh, I'm sorry, I've heard the question so many times I've got it backwards. What is the responsibility of the contemporary writer to prevent a war that will destroy the world and the human race.

MOUSTACHE

Of course, of course. But really getting it backwards isn't such a big mistake, at that. In fact I prefer the question backwards. What is the writer's responsibility?

MARTHA

To prevent war.

DEVIL

So there they are of a June night riding a limousine of sorts to the Jewish Theatre in Warsaw, talking away, talking away as all of us do, if I may include myself among the rest of you, and if I don't what is the good of that, really? We all know that the biggest achievement of the human race has been for at least a million years the putting of language of one sort or another into the voices and mouths of every human being alive, and this is a rather large achievement if you will stop to think about it for a moment. Here you are, gathered together in a theatre, and so you are not talking, you are listening to me and to the others in this play. Or you are reading the play and again this action of reading has stopped you from talking, but if you are a loud reader then whatever you are reading you are also speaking, you are at this very instant, for instance, saying, At this very instant. That is what art is, you know. The thing itself, and then the thing itself remembered—or something like that. What do I know? I am only this silly red-tailed invention that is supposed to signify the enemy—of everything good, as if it could possibly be possible—yesssss, folksssss, I mean precisely possibly be possible—for anything to be good without me, without bad, but now they are at the Jewish Theatre and the curtain has gone up and they are looking and listening from center seats not in the first row which is crowded but in the last row which is in another world, almost. The house is not packed. Indeed there are only two hundred people in a theatre with eight hundred places, so the Armenian traveler and the Polish interpreter are separated from the rest of the audience, up front, down front, as near to the stage as possible, so that they can almost enter into the play itself, enter into the drama of living, that is to say, the beautiful drama of memory, of confusion, of fear, of sorrow, of pain, of comedy, of laughter, of glorious laughter in spite of agony everywhere. . . . And look who's talking please.

MOUSTACHE

The audience, are they Jewish people?

MARTHA

Well, I think so, but maybe some are not. The language is Jewish, but the people who hold the phone to their ears, or wear the phone, they hear a translation into Polish, of course.

MOUSTACHE

Are there Jewish people who do not speak or understand Jewish—or Yiddish, the language of Isaac Bashevis Singer, the great writer who accepted the Nobel Prize for Literature not long ago speaking in the Yiddish language, one of the most exciting events of recent years. Are there Jews who have become assimilated, or almost assimilated as we all know there are perhaps a million Armenians in Poland who have become assimilated, although many of them still acknowledge that they are Armenian.

MARTHA

I don't know, but maybe there are such Jews, but of course tourists come to this theatre and if they are from America they can wear the ear-phones and have the action put into English. You can also, if you wish.

MOUSTACHE

No, I must hear precisely what the Jewish people hear, that is the idea, you see. I mean, perhaps I ought to explain, for the past forty or more years I having been trying to feel the Jewish experience in relation to the holocaust.

MARTHA

Why?

MOUSTACHE

Because I am an Armenian, but as I did not experience the Armenian holocaust of 1915 because I was in America in California and was too young, seven years old, even to begin to understand it and then too busy running after my own meaning until the beginning of the Jewish holocaust, in 1934, let's say, the year of the publication of my first book, I decided by God I have got to try to understand, the millions dead have got to be understood one at a time, and the millions who killed the millions have got to be understood also, and indeed they are the millions who are so difficult to understand. The Turks, that is, and then the Germans. If it is hideous to be killed, is it not even more hideous to kill? Well, the question is no good at all, is it, because anybody not yet killed only wants to avoid being killed and any killer only wants to kill and go home to supper—it is really hideous, and that's why I am here instead of at that P.E.N. Club.

MARTHA

There are more Jews now in the world than before the holocaust,
I have heard. There is at least that small comfort, is there not.
And they say that we would not have an Israel today in the world
if there had not been the holocaust. I believe I have Jewish blood,
you know.

MOUSTACHE

Of course, of course, everybody does, especially Germans. And
Armenian blood runs through the veins of the Turks, or so we
say, don't we? While the dead, the dear dead say nothing,
nothing.

SCENE 2

MOUSTACHE

Now, here we are, at the birthplace of Frederic Chopin and
after an enormous lunch we shall hear a concert in the garden.
The house and garden are supposed to mean something
connected to Chopin's genius and we are none of us really
determined or even slightly willing to suggest that any house
any garden any place would have some connection with the
genius of anybody.

MARTHA

They say he was very devoted to the landscape here. They say
he used to wander in the woods for hours and then come home
and sit at the piano and play the most beautiful music anybody
ever heard.

MOUSTACHE

How right they are to say what they say, and all I can say is
I wish I could hear just one of the improvisations of the great
man as a small boy, for let us remember that he composed and
performed his first concerto when he was only nineteen. I mean,

is any composer in the world putting on tape piano improvisations of any kind at all?

MARTHA

Oh, yes, everybody puts on tape everything, you know. I have heard it said that while rehearsing even a great conductor puts everything on tape, but he himself does not study the tape, technicians study it, and I suppose they learn something from it, too. And then sometimes during a rehearsal a special effect in music is achieved by accident, perhaps, and this is isolated and presented to the conductor, the maestro, and he listens to it again and again, and he tries to have the orchestra make that same musical effect—but an accident is not always easy to do again, it is an accident, and how it happened, nobody knows.

MOUSTACHE

Martha, little Mudlark of Warsaw, you are a marvel, that's what you are, and only twenty-two years old and the mother of a son and a daughter, I thank Poland for selecting you to be my interpreter and companion.

MARTHA

I thank Poland for my life, and Finland for my little girl's life— Oh, what a story. But now we are at the birthplace of Poland's greatest son, so we must learn everything we can about him in a short time, must we not? His father was French, you know, but came to Poland as a young man in search of employment, and found a wife, and think of it, from that came Chopin and the music we all love.

MOUSTACHE

Yes, it is a great story, and as you may have heard me say perhaps two minutes ago for long years I find it desirable, I find it necessary, I find it imperative for some reason to listen to Chopin whenever I myself am Chopin, if you won't mind my putting it that way, for there is in every man it seems to me a side which is indeed Chopin, there is no other way to put it, and this side does not get things done, it is the side that reflects and broods and sorrows and yet somehow in the end it always turns out that in these brooding activities a man has been renewed, has been restored, he is once again himself, his old self, as the saying is, the fool he was born, and he can stop brooding and start charging the enemy again. He can start doing again, being, making, and especially believing, believing, believing.

MARTHA
Believing? Do you mean there is no believing in Chopin?

MOUSTACHE
Precisely. That is why the stuff is irresistible. And is totally bereft of any such bourgeois sentiment. It is anti-belief. And how the piano became the device for the expression of so much disbelief, rejection, indifference, and opposition to everything energetic and ambitious, that is something I find absolutely beautiful. But then the piano itself is beyond accounting, it is the marvel of the sound world, the universe of harmony and architecture, mathematics and language by means of little words of sound and rhythm, all of it solely itself, impossible to translate into any other language. And this man Chopin came along and made the piano his own and put to shame all of the other composers, but anybody at the piano, even a lunatic such as myself can say things by striking the keys that cannot be said in any other way. But Chopin's way—wow, if I were Chopin I would play it, but I cannot say it, it cannot be said. Poland is the country of the piano to me, but I am enchanted by Copernicus and whenever we drive past the statue to him, in the center of Warsaw somewhere, my very soul smiles— Copernicus is holding a globe with an outer body representing space and universe, and he is young, and he knows that everything we know is like a grain of sand on an endless beach. That delights me. Everybody else in science and religion and philosophy thought we knew everything. I know I did—until I was eleven.

107

MARTHA

I didn't. I always knew I was very ignorant.

MOUSTACHE

That's not so. You are very bright. You are Polish.

SCENE 3

SAROYAN

Here I am again, myself, or something like myself, and I am not going to go into this matter of who and how and all, President Nixon, so to put it, is said to have tried something of the sort in the book he wrote, for which Irving Lazar, called Swifty, fetched him a cool, or perhaps hot, or at any rate possibly lukewarm, million dollars. And Pirandello, who never so much as thought of being President, not even of Italy, or Monaco, or Andorra, or Lichtenstein, where clever hustlers, frequently Greek, situate themselves and ever after never pay taxes, Pirandello went into the dimension of identity rather cleverly in some of his plays, so all I really need to say is here I am, myself, the writer, and what I want to say is this: it's happening, it is actually happening, as I write, as you read, or as you behold a performance of this play, this document of travel and transaction, this is happening, whatever it is, it is indeed happening, and that is the marvel of art, for at best all of this happened quite a few weeks ago as I write, possibly quite a few years ago as you read or witness the performing of this, and I wonder who is playing the part of Saroyan. Well, whoever it is, good luck to him, I had good luck pretty much all the way, or certainly so far, and never mind the cancer part, so everybody has got to have something and there is cancer in the Saroyan family, both sides, the father's kid brother died of it in Fresno at the Veterans Hospital, and the mother's mother died of it somewhere in a kind of hospital rest-home in Dinuba or Reedley or Kingsburg or somewhere not far from Fresno. A tribe will have cancer in its chemistry for centuries and it will do the job of allowing passage out, and then all of a sudden cancer will be discovered and Walter Winchell on national radio will raise at least 500 million dollars in the name of his pal Damon Runyon, but cancer, folks, was always there and always did the job, always permitted passage. It is happening, this writing is happening as I stand at the easel in the flat in Paris, Christ I came here twenty years ago, where did the pigeons go, so to put it, where are the neighborhood eccentrics of 1960, boys and girls, where is the jolly *clochard* who opened his arms to all pretty girls and scared them half to death—nobody wants the humor of a wino, not even in Paris—where did the money go? It went to the Tax Collector, that's where. And where is the star of the story going. You've heard of Death and Taxes. Well, that's where. The money to the Tax Collector, the star to Death, and so be it, so be it, you're doing just fine, and that's what counts. I am here again to suggest that it is time to go back just a short time to a talk with one of the gentlemen in Warsaw attached to the American Embassy, the Chief Culture Officer, if that is the proper or even only appropriate designation for him. And you couldn't find a nicer man if you searched the streets of Charleston for a long time, by name Roger. But let Moustache, as he is called, take over, you've had enough of me, by God, I do have a certain reticence, you know, and while Moustache is also me in the play, whether performed or only read, he is himself, first an actor, second a variation of myself—or as we used to say, me, myself, and I.

ROGER

You spoke well, you spoke very well tonight, everybody during the champagne party afterwards kept telling me they had never heard anybody speak the way you spoke. They said it might have been Mark Twain they were hearing. What you said was full of surprises and of course many jokes and much laughter—I mean, you didn't laugh, on the contrary, but everybody listening laughed, there were three hundred or more and frequently at these affairs we feel lucky if we get forty or fifty, and we have got to see to it, to get them. How much of what you said was written? You didn't seem to be reading a speech—and everybody does that these days.

MOUSTACHE

I write and I talk also for myself, if not indeed more for myself than for a listener or a reader. I do what I do. I don't know how to do anything else. I cannot, I will not write a speech, because I do not ever have to be concerned about saying something wrong. I have nothing that might be considered unsuitable information to pass along to the enemy, and of course you understand that I do not believe in an enemy. I made some notes, though, because almost invariably I forget to pay my respects to the kind people who have invited me, and so on.

ROGER

Well, of course we invited you, and they also invited you, and we and they were delighted that you could accept. So far what do you dislike about the Program? We try to make it right, but we know we fail.

MOUSTACHE

For fifty years I traveled alone. This is the first time I am a member of a group of American writers. Never again.

SAROYAN

Well, let it stand, then, but there is this to be said, and I mean by me, the writer, not by an actor or a director or an editor or a publisher but by me standing at the typewriter and putting it all down: drawing closer every day to the end I am of course more intensely than ever concerned about art. I want to know what it is. And I am finding that it is just as inaccessible, as the word goes, to understanding as ever. Perhaps it does not need to be understood, precisely as in the end life itself does not need to be understood, and meaning, if I may be forgiven, does not need to have any real meaning. The talk was given at the end of a week-long confabulation of English teachers in a holiday place on a lake about forty-four miles south of Warsaw, and the program had originally taken me there for the full week but I had refused saying, Gentlemen, no, I have never visited a resort in my life, I don't mind nature at all, but mixing nature with a lot of hourly discussions by a lot of English teachers would drive me up a wall. When you want me to make my talk, let a chauffeur take me to that place, let it be early in the afternoon of the evening when I shall talk and after the talk let the chauffeur take me back to Warsaw and my room at the good old Europejski Hotel, for that is home to me these days and nights. But the chauffeur drove me down at two in the afternoon and the Cultural Program Director, Roger Devonshire, for instance, drove me back in the same Ranch Wagon after the champagne party, after the talk, and so there was time to drive along and to chat. Let us chat as we chatted a month or so ago, or whatever it was, for it is true, we chatted.

ROGER

Never again? Really? Why not? I mean, you get along so well with everybody. At least everybody thinks you do. We'd like to have you back.

MOUSTACHE

Well, just invite me, and we'll think about it, but be sure to tell me first of all that I shall be no part of any group, I shall be invited solely alone, for had I known that I would have to stand around waiting for five or six other American writers to get into a bus at nine in the morning, but only I am there at nine, and at ten only two others are there, and at eleven at last coming along real elegantly is the last of the writers—what am I doing waiting, in Warsaw. I can't wait in Fresno, why should I wait in Warsaw? And why have I been kept waiting, why hadn't the writers come to the bus at nine o'clock, and those who didn't make it until ten, why hadn't they made it?

ROGER

Well, you know, one of them had asked the hotel desk to call him at eight but they hadn't called him.

WARSAW VISITOR

MOUSTACHE

Big deal. If the schedule is nine and there are five or six people involved, it is necessary, that's all, just plain necessary for every one of the five or six people to be at the stupid bus at nine o'clock or to make known that they shall not go. I hate being kept waiting—by Christ, if Jesus were to keep me waiting, I would convert to Islam. How, exactly, did he walk on water?

ROGER

What? I mean, I wasn't listening as carefully as I should have been, I suppose. Walk on water? Who? Jesus? I have never given the matter any thought. I have always presumed that he did, that's all. I suppose levitation of some kind. Or possibly a deliberate piece of illusion, of magic. Are you a fan of magic? I mean, I want to talk some more about the Program, but somehow talking with you other matters come up.

MOUSTACHE

No, I am not a fan of magic and I consider everybody who is a fan of magic a kind of nitwit, like Orson Wells, for instance, who even likes to perform magic, or fraudulence. I am fascinated by miracle, however. I want whatever happens to happen, not to be a lie, not to be an illusion. A tiger comes out of an empty box that is quickly shut and turned around. That's magic, it bores me. If a mouse really came out of the stupid box the stupid magician himself would faint away—because there was not supposed to be a mouse in the stupid illusion. Don't expect me to put up with writers who can't meet a nine o'clock bus schedule, and I don't care what they write or what their schooling has been.

ROGER

They spoke to the English teachers as you did tonight.

MOUSTACHE

Thank Christ I was in Warsaw. They are all so proud of referring each of them to "my psychiatrist." My thumb in my mouth?

Is that what they are saying, for Christ's sake? And yet they win prizes and are paid homage at big national televised parties in Washington! These are the people who are the enemies of art, that's all, and I want no part of them, ever.

ROGER

Ah, you know you don't mean that. They are the best we have.

MOUSTACHE

Maybe so. But they are terrible bores, too.

SCENE 4

MOUSTACHE

This is the Jewish Cemetery, it's out a bit but not far from the Catholic Cemetery and from a couple of other cemeteries but I do not believe I have ever heard of a cemetery for the Armenians, alone, although in Fresno there is Ararat Cemetery, and having been filled over the past half century, or all lots sold at any rate, the Armenians bought another piece of vineyard and called it Massis, which is how Ararat stands where it stands, the big mountain and the lesser mountain beside it, and that is how it is in Fresno, but here in Warsaw the problem could not be solved in any such simple manner—jump the S.P. railroad tracks adjoining Ararat and transform another vineyard into Massis. Here the procedure was to put the graves eight deep— and that is rather deep, surely far deeper than the six feet of song and legend to which all bodies (in all caskets) are consigned. But it surely took some maneuvering among the owners of the cemetery plot in old Warsaw to work things out. From the birthplace of Chopin, then, to the burial place of the man who invented Esperanto. Yes, he is in here along with surely twenty-two thousand other fascinating men and women— although the emphasis is altogether on the men. Is that traditional among the people of Moses, Martha? Ask the caretaker.

WARSAW VISITOR

MARTHA

I already know, this is not my first visit to the Jewish Cemetery,
and I know the caretaker from each of my previous visits. Yes,
it is traditional, but only because lately it has not been
commonplace for Jewish women to be very much more than
wives and mothers. But even if a Jewish woman had
achievement, important achievements for the Jewish people,
the caretaker says it would be her father or husband whose name
would be on the plot. But why have you come to the Jewish
Cemetery of Warsaw, you are an Armenian, why do you not
look for Armenian graves?

MOUSTACHE

What nonsense, dear child. The dead are the dead, it is true
of course, and a Jew is a Jew, and an Armenian is an Armenian,
and a Pole is a Pole, but a living body is a living body and a
dead body is a dead body. I go to cemeteries everywhere and
I am fascinated by the love and other things in the hearts and
minds of the survivors which impels them to spend great sums
of money and considerable thought on the stones. Which is most
important—the man, the body in which he lived, the life he lived,
the funeral, the place in the cemetery, the position in the place
eight-deep, the stone, or what is carved upon it? Don't answer,
there is no answer, it is all important and permits travelers from
the far corners of the world and the great distances of time to
come and gawk, to stare, to study, to read, to ruminate, to try
to guess the truth of it all. I have come to the Jewish Cemetery
in Warsaw to honor the indestructibility of the Jewish people
in the dispersion, invited to Poland as they were, and as the
Armenians were, and yet hated by those sad innocents who are
forever explaining their hardships by putting the cause upon
everything and everybody excepting themselves and their own
government, so to put it. And I have come here to see my own
burial place, my own grave, my own tombstone. All, all, all
that I have seen here fills my soul with pride and joy. There
is no death, there is interruption. There is death and it is final,

it is death, and none of us shall come again, so make the most of your nickel's worth of time and opportunity.

MARTHA

The caretaker wants to know what you are saying.

MOUSTACHE

Well, tell him, dear child. I am here to pay homage to myself by paying homage to the Jews who came to Warsaw or were born in Warsaw and worked in Warsaw and were rewarded for their hard work and their good achievements in Warsaw and who sickened in Warsaw or suffered an accident of one sort or another in Warsaw and died in Warsaw and were buried in Warsaw. Had there been a place for each of them in Israel would they have instructed the family to bury them there? I don't think so. Wherever a Jew is buried is Israel, and that is why I am here. And Jews are buried everywhere, in open dignity, as here, but in secrecy and disguise in many other places, but all of the places are Israel, if they lived by the law.

MARTHA

He says you sound just like an elder.

MOUSTACHE

How kind he is, and really majestic. Yesterday back in the halls of learning and exchange of culture one of the American writers who had visited here the previous day said that the caretaker seemed to be straight out of the writings of Franz Kafka, but that turns out to have been some kind of snobbism for this man is straight out of the pages of himself, or at best, or worst, of Singer or Babel. Sir, my friend, I thank you.

MARTHA

Oh, that is too much. You gave him too much, much too much.

DEVIL

What ranting, what raving, what nonsense, what folly, and really why, I must ask, why is so much made of the strange customs of human beings about the dead. And what strange inventions for himself, he he he himself, after he leaves his flesh. And his bones and his blood and bile and his chemical factory and the simple truth of his breathing apparatus. The man is dead, his body is nothing, everything he was is now nothing, it is gone, it is ended, and yet great rituals attend the disposition of the poor useless inert rotting body. Well, it's true, the thing begins to rot the instant the breathing stops and the apparatus has no power at all. But on and on the poor things go, inventing and believing, inventing and believing. And what inventions, what astonishing inventions of all kinds.

MOUSTACHE

Hold on a minute, Red Tail. That rhythm brings to mind, and memory, and music, something I want. Inventing and believing, inventing and believing, what was it that was put into a great, if unknown, if secret, American song with a rhythm of that kind. Ah, here it is, and I thank you, heavenly memory. Hugging and a chalking, hugging and a chalking, a crazy American song, by good old Hoagy Carmichael.

MARTHA

Song? Who is this man. Hoggy you say? Carmiachael you say? We are now at the Catholic Cemetery and you seem to be talking to somebody also, not me, and to be listening to words I can't hear, is that possible? What are you talking about in the cemetery which John Paul himself so frequently visited before he became the Pope? Hugging and what. What did you say? I mean, it is part of my work and nature to want to learn. Why did a song come into your head at a time like this?

MOUSTACHE

Not my head, or not my head alone, but into my ear, and into memory. Old Red Tail—he's myself, you know, who could he possibly be, and yes, you can't see or hear him, for you have your own of his kind and you can see and hear your own, and I can't—old Red Tail he was talking his usual nonsense, precisely like my own usual nonsense, and suddenly he said something that rang a bell, as we say, he said inventing and believing, meaning religion itself and something like accepting as truth that which is desirable as expectation, and he said it again, inventing and believing, and put me back forty years or so when I heard a strange lively song that made no sense at all but was absolutely delightful to hear.

MARTHA

A song? What kind of song?

MOUSTACHE

Well, you see, what it was was this enormous girl, like somebody in a Circus Sideshow, very big, beyond belief almost, and quite amorous, as the word has it, and there was this small man, a man not unlike the writer of the song, Hoagy Carmichael himself, the man who wrote ''Old Rocking Chair'' and a dozen great classic American popular songs and this man fell in love with this huge woman and wanted to embrace her, but of course she was too big for that. Perhaps you have seen people trying to put their arms around a Redwood Tree in California. Six or seven of them can finally make it, and that is how it was with Hoagy Carmichael or the lover in his song. He had to stretch his arms out and with chalk mark his place, and do it again until he had worked his way around the large mass of woman and all of it amorous, and not too much for the little man with the arms, the chalk, and the passion. Not to mention the laughter. He hugged and chalked and sang about his passion, saying everything that had to be said. And that is the song I am hearing right now and I wish you could hear it, too, for it is one of the truly hilarious songs of the world—neglected, unknown, performed once or twice on radio but never on television or in a movie because sober heads always prevailed and claimed it was silly. There was no such woman, there could not be, what would people think, and so on? But as far as I am concerned she is life itself and everybody is her lover and is forever a-hugging and a-chalking to get his arms around her for one big loving embrace, which of course cannot be managed, life is too much, the fat girl is too big, all that any man can do is hug and mark and sing as he goes, and that is what I am doing.

MARTHA

I had heard you were funny, but I didn't expect this. What do you mean? What are you saying? Hugging and chalking? Chalking? Talking?

MOUSTACHE

Every writer has got to make the most of his songs, for they connect deepest and best to his reality. His rhythm, his vitality, his reality, and all of a sudden Hugging and Chalking tells it all for me.

MARTHA

But it is silly, it is a silly song.

MOUSTACHE

Dear child, please do not belittle Christianity, please do not ridicule Moses, Jesus, Mohammed, and all of the others, all of us.

SCENE 5

SAROYAN

Here I am again, and there is a reason, I believe, for now I myself, the Warsaw Visitor, am wandering around not far from my niche or cell in the grand Europejski Hotel, and nobody is with me. Nobody excepting the world and the people in the streets of the world. Sir, excuse me, can you tell me how to reach the address written down on this piece of paper? The place

is the Jewish Museum, and having visited the Jewish Cemetery
yesterday, today I want to visit the Jewish Museum and as soon
as possible the main synagogue for I am an Armenian born eight
or nine or ten thousand miles from my ancestral home in the
Highlands, and isn't it said that one Jew can outwit three Greeks
but that one Armenian can outwit three Jews. Good God, I never
got that story straight. The idea is that the Armenians are the
cleverest people in the world. Well, it isn't that this is a lie,
it is simply that the element of truth in it is not isolated and
given proper relationship to the larger truth—namely, that most
Armenians are not clever at all but that a few of them are fairly
clever if given an easy opportunity. In other words, the story
is fantasy, but it holds on and on and on, and I think of Armenak
my father and how unclever he was every day of his busy and
sad 38 years. How many Greeks could Armenak outwit? How
many Jews? Why, the man couldn't outwit a blade of grass,
if you will permit the absurd parallel, but I get hot when I am
reminded that since I am an Armenian I must be very clever
and anybody doing business with me must be very careful. If
I had the right Armenian saying, I could say a word or two
about being able to outwit the very Angel of Death and to deceive
him into believing I was not his man, but my enemy was his
man, and send the Angel of Death to take him instead of me.
I could do that, by God. I could deceive the Angel of Death
into committing a big fat *faux pas.*

DEVIL

Did somebody mention my name?

MOUSTACHE

You are not the Angel of Death, old boy, you are a joke out
of the lore of that Ageless Angel perhaps, and get thee hence,
please.

DEVIL

You seem to be wandering around aimlessly, perhaps I can help
you. If you want the Jewish Museum, that building straight ahead

is on the street named on the slip of paper you keep showing to strangers, and it may have the precise number you seek, if buildings would bother to put up their numbers, so why don't you go there and find out what it is.

MOUSTACHE

Good thinking, old nitwit of my soul, how often over the long crowded and lonely years you have sent me into the silliest places ever put up in the world on the theory that each of them was the gateway to truth itself, and what each was, like as not, was a whorehouse—mystic, mystic, mystic, the white female body in there, scented and warm, round and hearty, or cool and fragile, for hire, and hardly ever beyond the means of the sojourner. Or if not a whorehouse, a gambling house, with watching eyes of thieves beholding the arrival of the lamb, the Lord's own Innocent, and then a sudden burst of cordiality, Come, come, sit down, of course we are all your friends, here is Leo, here Max, here Sam, here Joe, what'll it be, it's on the house, and no strings attached, and if you wish to take a hand of cards the stakes are for you to decide, nothing too small, nothing too large and everything over and above board—honesty we have always believed, is the best policy, or in the French of Willie Howard, the best policement. Yes, I'll go into that grand edifice right there and I may as well say I shall not be shocked if it turns out to be a daytime sleepy whorehouse or a gambling house betimes, as the word goes. I am out in Warsaw to pass the afternoon in dignity and earnestness, the visiting of a golden building is a good thing, always, I understand.

DEVIL

Like the saying goes, if you're lost, there is always a profit in loss, and whatever the building is, it is, is it not. Go on in, What is it.

MOUSTACHE

By God, there's the most famous face in the world: Lenin. It's the Lenin Museum of Poland, of Warsaw, set up by Moscow soon after the hugging and chalking of Poland into the Soviet body, so to put it, but bereft of visitors, not one Pole in the place, only the staff of big patient Russian women, and how astonished and pleased and yet slightly annoyed they are by my arrival, hurrying from place to place, switching on electric lights, revealing great displays of memorabilia of Lenin in Poland and everywhere else—what a piece of good luck this is, really. I have always loved the good brave man, for he went to the Caucasus and he knew the Armenian Communists and there are photographs of them standing with him. Such things matter, this is indeed a joy: the unclever Armenians.

DEVIL

Let's just say for the devil of it ha ha ha I am the Devil so just for the devil of it let's say I am one of the big big and man I mean big big BIG journalists of the world and I want to interview you, what would you say to that, and just remember we are in the Lenin Museum in Warsaw not the Public Library in Fresno. There is a difference.

MOUSTACHE

There is no difference whatsoever. We are who we are wherever we happen to be and right now the Lenin Museum is where we happen to be and here comes the big Russian character in one of the lazier of the short stories of one of Russia's lazier writers, let's say Andreyev, let's say Gorky, but let's not say Chekhov, and this great hulk of a lady has come to do two things: switch on a light and spy, the traditional activity of Soviet Communism, let us say, but why not also of American Capitalism if we are going to be mean about it? So go ahead, interview.

DEVIL

Well shall I be, an interviewer of great courtesy or an interviewer of great discourtesy? I mean, you know perfectly well that if there is one thing Satan's worldwide international universal nonpareil agents have it is mercy, it is gentility, it is courtesy, but if you might take a notion in your head that you would like a kind of duel, then of course I can be savage, too. I was always careful in my reading of every interview by Oriana Fallaci that ferocious little woman who exposed everybody she ever talked to—Henry Kissinger, the Ayatollah Khomeini, Jesus of Nazareth, Frank Sinatra, and Pope John Paul. I know how she does it, but I have never quite understood why. I mean, she hates everything hateful in life, and that compels my admiration, but she also seems to hate everything that is not hateful and indeed is rather lovable in life, in survival, in behavior, in people, in herself, especially in herself, dear clever girl.

MOUSTACHE

Stop your yammering, Sir, I say Sir, stop it. Here's Mikoyan in an early photograph with his pal Stalin, and what jolly lads they are, determined to change the world as soon as possible, and by God for one time in the history of change these lads did not fail, the Armenian and the Georgian, they did indeed change the world—it would have changed by itself and perhaps less stupidly, but it was fun for them while they were at their work, and in the end nobody knows the difference. Everything happened, and then the Georgian died of a stroke and years and years later the Armenian died of something or other and everything goes right on happening as if they hadn't changed the world, hadn't lived in fact—and what killings the Georgian quietly, casually demanded, what executions of what innocents. By the hundreds, by the thousands, by the millions, never mind the executions that came about of themselves in heroic war, for all of the Russians and peoples of the Soviet family of peoples fought the enemy to the death, and Russia lives and Germany lives, and Communism of some sort continues to sicken while whatever you want to call that which Germany was afflicted with, Nazi-ism or Hitlerism or Fascism or Anti-Semitism or anti-humanism or whatever, that also continues to die and resurrect and sicken and die, for all of it, all of it is us, it is not somebody else. Young Anastas Mikoyan—well, I never knew another Armenian who had been given the name Anastas, and as for Mikoyan itself, the way that happened, and a good thing, is that the name of his father was Mukkerditchian, and so they called the young shaver Muko for short, which was sometimes both pronounced and heard as Miko, Miko became Mikoyan, and he would have been the same man in any part of the world, any country, functioning under any economic political or cultural system, he would have been the wily little Armenian, as certain American journalists liked to call him, for he avoided the ax of his old pal Josef Stalin for a good half century while other intimates, old friends, were given the ax, and I mean in the neck. And that's why I say that Mikoyan changed the world as much as Stalin did, for the Armenian keeping himself alive and useful to the Georgian also passed along to the man in power all of the hints that permitted Russia finally to commit suicide and at the same time to not only survive but to be purged, like a lunatic in a Dostoyevsky novel. I hope I shall see other early snapshots of the victors over Trotsky in the struggle for power, and the victors also over Lenin, never mind how much honor is paid to the name of Lenin, for there has never been anybody in this world with so many portraits painted of his rather blunt face. As for his Tomb in Red Square I have twice visited it and looked upon the waxed face and hands of the man. And it won't do, except that it does do. Lenin is the hero of failed triumph.

DEVIL

All well and good, if very boring, but what are you thinking, Sir, I say Sir, to take a hint from your way of addressing me, are you thinking Death, is that it, everywhere you go Death, your own Death, and what I mean is, this is the first question of the interview.

MOUSTACHE

Yes, I am thinking Death, but I have always thought of Death. How could I possibly not have done so? It is there at the center of us and of everything up out into infinity of time and of place and space and down into the smallest units of action and being—

Christ, this sort of thing keeps happening to me and all it does is make me respect chess players, those bores of the world.

DEVIL

You do not respect chess players, Sir? I am surprised.

MOUSTACHE

What has respect got to do with it? Chess is a mathematical exercise in the achievement of glorious irrelevance and meaninglessness. All chess players are impotent. They are incapable of inhabiting their own bodies or joining the human family in the human world, and I speak of them only because I am forever going on out into the spheres with big stupid calculations of no use to me, to you, or to anybody else, precisely like the calculations of the chess players, masters and amateurs alike. The playing of the game is a joyful running away from the alternative—that is, living. It is sterile art. Nothing is produced from the intense concentration. It is an exercise in abstraction not put on paper in words of poetry or prose or on canvas in colors and relations or in music in sounds and rhythms or in dance or in paper cut-outs or in sculpture or in anything that brings something new, if only slightly so, out of anything already there—and that is what art is, of course. I suppose Lenin could play chess—who couldn't in his day—but I am willing to bet my very life that he avoided playing the game when he discovered the truth about it. Playing chess will neutralize the force and imagination in any man so that he will never need to make anything. What I mean is that even here in Warsaw on my first visit it annoys me that my thinking goes out and out to everywhere and nowhere and in and in to here and then so much more of here that it is identical with out and out, and I don't like this because in all of my years I have never found out how to make something out of this action, it is like a basic and stupid move in the earliest part of a chess game—and yet it happens to me all the time. I believe it must have something to do with everything, but especially with accident—birth, that is, my own, that is—and death, and again my own, of course, coming up, coming up, and this coming up of it for me is the reason I am in Warsaw in the first place. I do not want to both die inside and outside, or to put it another way I do not want to die in science as well as in art, in abstract and concrete truth, that is, cancer of the prostate, and in specific and personal truth, the self itself: and so when the Government itself, so to put it, invited me to visit Warsaw, I replied, Boys and girls, let me just finish this book I am writing, perhaps the most important of my whole career, "Adios Muchachos," Goodbye Children, So Long Kids, or whatever and I shall be glad to consider accepting your kind invitation. So I am here, for I did indeed finish the great book.

DEVIL

If it's so great, what's it about?

MOUSTACHE

Me. Saying goodbye.

DEVIL

If it's about you, what's so great about that?

MOUSTACHE

It is also about you, and yours, and me and mine as if it were you and yours, me and my stupid son and my stupid daughter and their stupid mother—thank God she found her proper place in the world and got out of my hair, wow, that was close—and about lies and deceptions and dishonor and dirt and sweet scents all over it all as a soft open sexual body to receive the seed and continue the children, and about the saying of goodbye to them, in Spanish, in Mexican, Adios Muchachos, in other words, because I was born in Fresno, dead center of California, where the Mexicans lived long before the arrival of the pale skins with their Christian justification of slaughter, the systematic annihilation of everybody in the way, and so I know the faces of the kids, the muchachos of the Mexicans, the Indians, the half-breeds, the mestizos, and I like the crazy tango that was given that name and to which so many of the dancing Armenian boys of Fresno sixty years ago took into their arms so many of the daughters of everybody else and swooped about and dipped and whirled and tried to hide their erections. And so I finished the great book and I came straight to Warsaw. So here I am, am I not, in the Lenin Museum.

DEVIL

Well, don't go berserk, please, plenty of time for that, most likely, when you up and die, I suppose that is the time to fly apart, to go to pieces, to be shattered back into the universe as you like to put it, helplessly as you say. I was only asking. What do I know. But what is more useful to the interview is, What do you know?

MOUSTACHE

Well, I know I'm dying, and that is the one thing we are really prohibited from knowing—nature does it so that we shall first do our natural work and then whenever the accident happens we may perhaps notice, and know, that we are dying and that there is no longer forever as there had always been the illusion that there was. I have always known only that which all living things in the human branch of the animal family have known— that I am, I breathe, I move, I remember, I think, I rejoice, I despair, I sleep, I dream, I become restored, I find a new day not too much for me, I get up, I start out, I become tired, sometimes I become exhausted as I am at this very moment from having had so many days and evenings and nights of talking, talking, listening with my deaf hearing, listening and trying to understand the talk and the questions of the writers of Warsaw, and the University students of Warsaw, and the members of the Party of Warsaw, and the enemies of the members of the Party of Warsaw, the secret enemies, the underground boys and girls, the brave lads and lasses, listening and watching and waiting—to take back Poland, to wrench it away from Russia, to have the people and the land equal one to the other, to evict the invaders, to be truly Poles again—and it will happen very probably but not in my time for there is no time left in my time. So I stand here over this glass showcase in the Lenin Museum and I study the endless memorabilia of the great man and his great comrades, and I think and think, Christ, so let us say the Poles wrench Poland out of the embrace of Russia, and Poland is Poland again, so what is the difference? And I know the question is rude and really stupid, but at the same time I also know that it must be asked, for the answer tells us something we have always known but somehow have never cared to really know.

DEVIL

And what is that, pray tell, Sir, I say Sir, what is that?

MOUSTACHE

Well, let me see how to put it. The fact is that in his heart every man knows that all he is is himself and everything outside of that truth is so much theory, however legendary it may be. In Afghanistan at this very moment those good people are gladly dying for their geography, they are being killed in mortal combat with the Russians, but actually only with themselves, for there are quite a few Marxists and Leninists and Soviet Communists among them so that the taking up of arms against the invader is the taking up of arms against the self—and the self is all, Afghanistan is part of the self of course, but a comparatively small part of it, the great part of the self is the part that does not permit itself to be too well known. Who is the enemy if not the self and the selves of the father and mother and the brothers and sisters and the sons and daughters?—all of this truth kept decently as far from light and intelligence as nature demands, and it does an excellent job. In the end the Afghanistan people will adjust to having been in the Soviet Russian family of nations and they will consider heroes the men who are now considered traitors. It happens wherever Soviet Communism goes and it is desirable for us to be charitable about the wishy-washy intensity of everybody about who they are, for each person is only himself, and Christ Almighty if the way out of that terrible predicament is to betray the self, what could possibly be easier, and indeed more intelligent, useful, right?

DEVIL

And after making known that what you know is almost nothing better than the animals know, have you any concern at all for what the insects know? I mean, they have survived just as amazingly as humans have.

MOUSTACHE

I have indeed always found the reality of the insects absolutely admirable and even delightful, for it is delightful that for millions of years various kinds of insects continue to come into being for a total life-span of perhaps no more than half an hour, and during that time they do what all of the other survivors do to go on surviving—they breed and however unlikely that situation may seem to human understanding they manage it, and it works. Very little else works, but that conjunction of the parts of apparatus involved works, and the billion-year-old fragile insects consequently return next season and with their amazing half hour of—what shall we call it?—being, reality, truth, connection? Yes, let us call it each of those things, and then add all of the words of the dictionary.

SCENE 6

SAROYAN

There is something fishy about death. There is also something totally beyond us that perhaps ought not to be and might not be were it not that we took off when we did take off on the scientific investigation of the unknown rather than the other way. The scientific way is the consequence of insatiable greed—for information. It is by itself perhaps the most heroic reality in us. But it fails to work at all when it comes to death. Except of course in its simple physical form and meaning, and in that area, that dimension, we have a good full supply of information, all of it wrong, or slightly wrong, as indeed all information must be presumed to be. I mention this because I have got to mention something and because death has come to me. Oh, I'm still alive and still kicking, which means I am still fighting out each day's demands on me to survive and to make the most of every moment in Budapest, then in Bucharest, then in Belgrade, and finally back in my own flat in Paris, a flat I have occupied part of every year for twenty years—and still don't speak a word of proven French—in all of those places and among all of the activities in which I figured I was dying, I was indeed dead or as good as dead but still wandering around, and this is the part that keeps itself aloof from us—I have always been precisely what I have been and what I am at this very moment: who I am and what I am and how and all the rest of it has always been like this. I am here, I am myself, I am nobody else, I have my own as each of us has his own: body, heritage, sleep, meaning, style, character, truth, and if you like complications, untruth, unreality, unbeing and so on, simultaneously with the opposites of them—and there has not been, ever, any full deliverance from death, not the possibility of it, but the living reality of it in the very midst of the living reality of its opposite, everything I have just mentioned, and that is precisely how it is this instant, in Paris, on Thursday, the 26th of June, 1980, as I sip tea and stand at the typewriter and write these words which now either an actor is speaking or a reader, yourself, is reading. And I find it is permissible for me to go after whatever this is that is working itself out into some kind of addition to the little we have about ourselves near the end, and to get everything rather than more and more simple more and more impossible to make simple. We are fragile and can go, can be taken at any moment, but as long as we are not taken we are without doubt one of the most enduring orders of substances and actions that may exist or might be imagined as existing in the world, on earth, in the universe, and this is the part about death, about us, about our story, about our experience that I feel I have the obligation to speak about on the chance that I may just come up with something right and useful, for we know that the other way, the way of measure and factuality, so to put it, stops short at this point—that way can go no farther. We have measured everything related to birth and to death but we are still as far from knowing anything right and useful and real and glorious and hilarious and absurd and holy and sanctified and commonplace and ridiculous and preposterous and beautiful and innocent and right and right and right and not wrong not wrong not wrong about the fullness of the event of birth and the fullness of the event of death, and that is the reason I have come out here again to enhance rather than interrupt the play, which of course we all know is not a play at all, although anything is a play if we decide to say it is, is that not so? I have come out as myself because that seems to me to be the proper thing, as the writer of the play, to do. For instance, at random, do suicides really want to die? As well we might ask, Do foetuses really want to go on becoming final and full starting forms and to come out, to become born, to start the experience of being human for the billionth billionth time, let's say—the numbers have always confused me, and I really am suspicious of them, for *one* is the number that has still to be understood and is more than enough for our failure to know what may very well not be meant for fitting into meaning, or our notions of gathering of facts and understanding consequently let us say that which is not understandable—mystery, or truth in a dimension not permitted to animals, plants, minerals, oceans, continents, and all the rest of it. Does any man want to die? Want is the wrong wrong wrong word, most likely. If he doesn't really want to live, either, it does not change the probability that he never really wants to die. I know I don't, and I know I must, and so must each of us, so what, boys, girls?

MOUSTACHE
Here I am at the Jewish Museum. Do you like that? Even if you don't, here I am at the Jewish Museum.

DEVIL
I like it.

MOUSTACHE

Not you, I'm talking to time man time time time and place and person and travelers and especially the dead, the dead man, the dead of everybody, but most of all the dead of the Jews. Are they different from the dead of the Gypsies, for instance, and the Catholics, and the Anarchists, and the homosexuals, and the Communists, and the conspirators, and the thieves and assassins and saints and fools?

DEVIL

Yes, they are.

MOUSTACHE

Stay out of this if you don't mind.

DEVIL

I can't stay out of it. This is the Jewish Museum in Warsaw, is it not? And you were longer than an hour finding it, not counting the hour you spent in the Lenin Museum, and the reason you had to find the Jewish Museum is that the Jewish dead are different.

MOUSTACHE

Well, how do you come by that belief, pray tell, because I was about to say that they are different and now you've made me lose the train of thought by which I expected to characterise this difference. I feel it is in the Jewish children, for they have faces, especially eyes, that simultaneously accept and cry out in protest. I do not believe there have ever been more beautiful and heartbreaking faces upon the human being since the beginning of time than the faces of the Jewish kids, boys and girls alike, especially of Poland, of Warsaw, of Cracow, who were put to death at Auschwitz, which I expect to visit very soon—and yet somehow feel that I must not visit so that the memory of the faces of those children shall not be blurred by the architecture and terror in the various chambers of Auschwitz—chambers of horror inside buildings that could very

131

well be schools for instance or public buildings of various kinds. Why do you say the Jewish dead are different from the other dead also murdered at Auschwitz? Have you an answer, Sir, I say Sir?

DEVIL

Yes, Sir, I say Sir, and this is no time for you and me, or you and I, or you and you, or me and me, or I and I, to engage in these damnable word games, for while it is part of my work to track down whoever it may be on my assignment I have never been a party to such diseased programs of death as those of Buchenwald and Auschwitz, to name only two of surely twenty-two. I care for Gypsies and Anarchists and fools as much as any man or woman or child might care for anybody at all, but the Jewish dead who were murdered are different from all the others in that they were the human family at its most reasonable reality—for the purpose of decent continuance. Ah, no, no, that is not what I mean. What I mean is that the Jews feared God, whereas all of the others only loved God, if that, for we know many of them didn't even have a small willingness to even believe there could possibly be such a thing as God. God feared is greater than God loved, and the reason I say this is that I am one who fears God, and if I do not hate God, as I might be expected to do, I also do not love God. I am from the other side of the railroad tracks, am I not? God is supposed to hate me and my Commanding Officer, so to put it, and we in turn are supposed to hate God, but it is not so. God does not hate the Commanding Officer and he does not hate God, for if there was such hate then there is no telling what the consequences would be, for we do know that it was the hatred of much of the human race itself for the Jewish branch of it that made that branch so robust, so real, so right, so truly itself instead of the wishy-washy kind of thing all other branches of the human family tend to be, excepting perhaps those whose difference is unmistakable—the various tribesmen of Africa, and the various peoples of Asia. Europeans tend to look alike, and that's where the wishy-washy gets its greatest encouragement. There

are few Europeans who could not as easily be considered Italian
as Swedish, for instance, and such a situation is a continuous
invitation to wander away from the family, the fold, which the
Jewish people did not do because if they did there could be no
telling how filled with anguish and loss their souls would be—
and the Jewish people are the people who have always been
nearest to the human soul. That is how the Jewish dead are
different from all of the other dead murdered by the rest of us—
oh yes, we did it, we did it, it was not just the Germans, it was
not just Hitler and his big fat skinny sick brilliant stupid clever
dirty partners who always always only followed orders, as they
kept saying at the Nuremberg trials—it was us, old boy, us,
us, and I mean us.

SAROYAN

It is a sad state of affairs when a man's own self from the depths,
so to put it, the Devil, the Nemesis, the Killer, steps forward
and takes the words right out of the man's own mouth and the
emotions right out of his heart and makes a fool of himself and
of the man, but then that's life, as we say, and we had better
learn not to be too astonished by life or to fight it too bitterly.
Go on with the play, folks, whoever you are.

MOUSTACHE

What he said, what he tried to say, what he mumbled and
bumbled in English, not necessarily the appropriate language
for what he tried to say, or his own language, or the language
of anybody at all—let us try to think what Shakespeare would
have written in any of the other also inept and inappropriate
languages from Latin to Italian to Chinese and Arabic and Zulu
and Amharic and Urdu and pidgin English, and then let us
marvel at Shakespeare and not at English, for Shakespeare in
any language is Shakespeare. What old Red Tail tried to say
was that there can be differences between the various dead,
whether the varieties are racial, social, cultural, accidental, or
whatever. And in this Jewish Museum in Warsaw, closed for
repairs and restoration, in a shambles, I find the difference very

very difficult to speak about, and yet impossible not to feel. The Torah and the Menorah and the this and the that which have words and meanings unknown to me are here and the Scrolls and the Candles and the various cloths that are worn on certain occasions—all of the Hebrew things, all of the Jewish things will eventually be placed about in this Museum as well as the delineation of the history of the persecution and assassination of the Jewish people of Warsaw and Poland, and the survival of them. Poland means Jews. Poland means many things but it is never possible for Poland not also to mean Jews. Warsaw means Jews. And innocent Poland had many innocent Poles who half hated and half loved Jews but in the end were moved all the way over to the hate half and so very very little was done for betrayed people, although in private many great and beautiful things were done. Beside the door coming into this place is a small desk. Admission is free, but in any case there was nobody at the desk when I came in, but there will be a very nice woman of sixty or seventy, not skinny but also not fat, at the desk and I will stop to enquire without words if there is something I may buy as a souvenir of my visit to this place. She will find a copy of something and I will pay something or other for it and go out but now I am in the dust and gloom and sorrow and emptiness of this place, all in a shambles, and all of this permits me, compels me, to be a Jew, and a proud Jew, as if there could possibly be any Jew going to his destruction with hundreds and thousands of other Jews who would not be proud, who could possibly feel only something terrible about himself, like, All this, all this, all this for God's sake just for being Jewish? Is it that different? And who is doing this? What in God's name is he? Is she? For all of us take wives, do we not, and we get into bed with them and we exchange ourselves for a moment, the men becoming also women, and the women becoming also men, and afterwards the both of them living with the child-to-come and becoming mother and father to the child, and these men who are doing this, they have their wives, and there is the soft talk between them in bed and the women are not left out of this, they are part of it, and they are different, they are women, but they are not in that truth really different from the women who are Jews, and yet those women are here moving to their destruction while the other women are safe at home cooking cabbage and potatoes with sausages. I did not come to Warsaw in order to visit the Jewish Museum, in shambles during restoration but in a sense I am glad that I have reached this place in this condition while outside and all over the world the bright eyes and warm voices of the Jewish people living among themselves in Israel and among all of the other peoples of the world wherever they have their place and history, all of these survivors of the program of annihilation are brighter than ever—the holocaust has given the entire people a new grandeur of the universal, not of Jews alone but of everybody: hate us, kill us, you hate and kill yourselves, we are who you are, and you shall know this truth and cherish it for it shall touch your truth with the grandeur that came to us not in a light brushing of the wings of the angel of Death but in a collision with that angel in a million of its forms and in all of its forces. I apologize for these words. I was not destroyed in the holocaust. I am hushed and made proud in this place of dust and the continuation of the people of the Word to honor the Word.

SCENE 7

SAROYAN
Yes but what about Chopin's Walking Stick?

MARTHA
Yes, let's tell them how you came into possession of that wonderful black slim supple walking stick.

ROGER
Well, as Cultural Officer of Warsaw it seems to me that I ought to know all about such a thing, ought I not? Frederic Chopin's own walking stick? Really? Are you sure? It would be in the

house where he was born, wouldn't it? The Museum, or in some other historical cultural national place, wouldn't it? Where is it? How do you know it was his? Does it have a silver or gold head, perhaps carved in the shape of a piano, with his own signature under it. And a steel point.

MARTHA

Oh, yes, but better, far better than all that. But let him tell the story, I suppose, I was only tagging along at the time.

LISH

What is it?

MS RYE

Something about Chopin's own walking stick.

LISH

Did he have a walking stick? I don't remember ever having read of such a stick.

THE CEMETERY CARETAKER

Chopin? Walking stick? Where is he buried? I don't remember a stone for Chopin. Who is he?

MARTHA

No, no, old man. Frederic Chopin is not buried in the Jewish Cemetery of Warsaw, he is probably buried in Paris.

LISH

At Père Lachaise, I believe.

MS RYE

Really? I should have imagined that Poland would have insisted on having him buried at home.

MARTHA

He is, of course. He is deep in the hearts of all Poles, not just in Poland but all over the world. He is ours and we are his. We do not have such sentiments about Copernicus.

LISH

He wouldn't have wanted it.

MS RYE

How do you know? Perhaps a great scientist would enjoy being a favorite of the people even more than a great composer and performer of music on the piano. We have no way of being sure of such things, have we?

LISH

Quite so, my dear, quite right, quite true, but traditionally it seems to turn out that only the showy people seem to be embraced by everybody else, and sometimes for rather long spells. So far I have not heard anybody at all speak about Copernicus and anything he was famous for.

MARTHA

We have many, many more, not just Chopin and Copernicus: we have our great soldiers, as you know in America, for did they not go to your country and help you win your independence?

WOMAN FROM THE LENIN MUSEUM

Are you speaking of Comrade Lenin? It is true, it is every bit of it true, he is the hero of the revolution.

MARTHA

Oh, Mama, Mama from Vladivostok, how beautiful you are in your devotion to Russia and Siberia and perhaps even Mongolia by remembering the grandeur of comrade Lenin, but at this moment we are restricting our heroes to the geography and culture of Poland, only right here, right around Warsaw.

ROGER

Culture? Did somebody mention the word culture? I am all for
it, you know, but I must confess that some of the people that
Washington sends to me to engage in cultural programs are
sometimes a trial—some of them just don't have manners, that's
all, they just don't seem to believe in punctuality, in schedules,
in time-tables, and if the truth is told, they look upon the whole
Cultural Program of which they are supposed to be a part as
nothing better than a holiday, a vacation, an escape from their
usual day to day life, which even for people of the arts can be
pretty dull and routine. I mean, nobody seems to understand
that as Cultural Officer I am responsible for the realization of
the program and it takes doing, it really takes more doing than
I can manage. This is all just fine, just fine, but I have got to
see that the Americans make a good impression on the Poles,
and then I have got to hope that the Poles really understand
that the purpose of our Cultural Program is very simple—to
make known a little more about America.

MARTHA

Oh, we know, we know, and do you think we don't appreciate
such programs? We do indeed, all of us, perhaps even Chopin
and Copernicus.

MS RYE

What did she say? So many people turn out to have subtle
comedy in their souls. She is laughing at him, isn't she? And
at us?

LISH

Well, if she is, who cares? Let her have her little laugh.

MARTHA

I do not laugh at anybody in this whole world, why should I
laugh at Americans, all of a sudden. I have seen even Charlie
Chaplin movies.

LISH

What does that mean, I wonder.

MS RYE

Oh surely nothing?

DEVIL

I see a lot of people cluttering about. Did somebody kick the bucket while my back was turned. My boy, my man, myself, you might say, didn't give up the ghost did he while I went in search of a McDonald's in Warsaw, for I know there is no such place, but in looking for such a place one comes upon the equivalent of such a place, and now and then the snack they serve is almost as good as a hamburger. What's going on, I mean?

MOUSTACHE

There is this sudden concern about death in Warsaw, for we have all heard of *Death in Venice* and naturally Warsaw doesn't want to be left out of it, left out of the literature of death here and there, in certain circumstances—no, Sir, I say Sir, I am here, although at this moment back in my hangout in Paris doing my usual work, waiting for the symptoms to swarm all over everything and finish the job so I can say my last words. Look look look, is that light on the other side, all over again.

DEVIL

Are those your last words? Because if they are, I've heard better, but I've also heard worse and in any case they don't mean anything. They almost never do. It is a kind of small literary form, nothing more. And the party of the first part, about to become a stiff, he is almost never the speaker of the words, it is almost always somebody who imagined that he might have spoke them. So what's all the fuss about? Why is everybody all tense and hung-up in this manner, as if expectations of many kinds were real and might be fulfilled.

MOUSTACHE

It has been said that Chopin's walking stick came to light in Warsaw again, after apparently having been lost for a century or more, that seems to be what this is all about, if you can believe it.

DEVIL

I cannot, but I do, for in my line of work sooner or later you come to believe anything can happen. Walking stick? Chopin's? So what?

MARTHA

So what? Do you think it is a small thing that Chopin like Charlie Chaplin, whose movies I have seen, enjoyed holding a walking stick—very slim, very supple, very, how shall I say it, very agile, resilient. Charlie Chaplin's was bamboo, I believe, and if he put a little weight on it, it became bent, like part of a circle, and then when he removed the weight the stick became straight again, and he used the putting of weight upon it and the lifting of weight upon it to emphasize something he was doing, usually he would be flirting with a pretty girl or hoping to make a good impression on the grand dame who was blocking the way to the big party where there was food and champagne and where Charlie Chaplin wanted to go. There have been others who have carried such slim bamboo or other walking sticks, for they are manufactured by the thousands in various parts of Asia and sent all over the world.

MOUSTACHE

As a matter of fact, James Joyce is photographed holding such a slim stick, but made of hardwood it would seem, but standing beside him is James Stephens, and he does not hold such a stick—it is a great photograph. And of course there has never been a Fair anywhere in the world where bamboo and other walking sticks were not sold for a small coin or given to winners of small contests. Perhaps this is part of the reason it was desirable for me to come into possession of Frederic Chopin's own walking stick.

DEVIL

How did you do that, pray tell? I mean one takes a cherry from a box in a market when nobody is looking but surely you were not able to take a walking stick out of a glass showcase at a museum somewhere and I can't imagine that you would pay actual money for such a stick being offered by an antique dealer, for you would surely know the stick was not authentic, it was one of dozens of similar sticks sold to admirers of Chopin, but you wouldn't pay a dollar for such a stick—or would you?

MARTHA

Nothing like that at all. Shall I tell them what happened.

MOUSTACHE

Yes, I wish you would.

MARTHA

We were walking in the gardens of the house where Chopin was born, and under one of the trees was a fallen branch. And he stopped and picked it up and broke off the smaller branches of the main branch and then he brought out a pocket knife and whittled a point, and then he cut through the top and thick part, and then he put his weight on the black branch precisely the way Charlie Chaplin did in the movies, and I said, What is that? And he said, This is Frederic Chopin's own walking stick. That is how it happened. It is the truth.

LISH

What nonsense. And we were led to believe that something quite different had happened. Silly, really.

MS RYE

Really?

DEVIL

Yes, but where is it, where is it, where is this magic walking stick made out of a branch of a tree in the garden of the house where Chopin was born? What is the point of it? And don't make a pun anybody—the point is at the bottom of the stick. I would like to know the point of this whole gathering together of all of us as if in some momentous and vital celebration. And so you made a stick from a branch of a tree, so you had it during a number of walks in Warsaw, so what do you mean by that?

MOUSTACHE

It was a sword as well, Sir, I say Sir, it was a device of punctuation, it was a pointer, it was a way to emphasize, to turn over playing cards in the street to find out the number or face of the card, it was a device of sport and style—I have never seen anybody so much at ease as James Joyce in that photograph somewhere in Paris in 1928. But I have always rescued fallen branches in that manner and put them to work as if they might each of them be a royal staff, an ecclesiastical staff, and it has been fun, I must say.

DEVIL

What has? Sir, I say Sir, what has been fun?

MOUSTACHE

Having been born, having been sent by the American government to Warsaw in the 72nd year of my time and life, and having joined in the Cultural Program, and having found the branch that became Chopin's walking stick.

DEVIL

Well, where is it, let's have a look at it, shall we, shall we?

MOUSTACHE

Alas, no, we cannot, and that's that.

ROGER

No no no, please, what happened to the branch of the tree that you made into Chopin's walking stick, for it may be useful to the Culture Program, now and forever, as the saying goes.

MOUSTACHE

Well, I don't mind letting you know, but first the branch was not fallen from a tree of the garden of the house where Chopin was born. I said that because it was appropriate. I found the park where the Chopin Monument is, and on my way I found the branch and made the stick in the manner described by Martha Mularuk who was not even there, I put it that way writing all this weeks later in my flat in Paris, that is how writing is done, you know. And I carried the stick until I came to where the Monument was and the Sunday afternoon concert was in progress, and I carried the stick as I made my way directly to where I could behold the girl who was playing the piano and there was a place on a bench and I sat there and listened, and when the concert ended about ten minutes later—I had been searching for the place a full hour and I had arrived very late—people ran up to have the autograph of the pianist, so I did too, and she also jotted down the name of the piece that had repeated again and again a kind of ominous ripple that I have always enjoyed hearing. And so the stick went with me by airplane to the next Cultural Program assignment to Prague, and then to Budapest, and then to Bucharest, and finally to Belgrade, and in each of these cities I carried the stick and made known that to me it was Chopin's own walking stick, but at the Moskva Hotel in Belgrade I was given an outside room without air conditioning, at my request, but after one night I decided that I had better get another room for this room was too hot and the noises from the busy street were too loud. So I asked to have another room and the friendly man at the desk said, Tomorrow it will happen. And the next day he sent up a man who helped me move from 321 to 307 and this new room turned out to have a magnificent view of both the Sava and the Danube and of the New City and of the Park down below and I felt delighted and at home. Also, in the ice box full of bottles that one might enjoy, and pay for, on the bill, I found a neatly wrapped package containing two dozen each of excellent elegant expensive pastries, and this was not a gift from the management, it was something either forgotten by the previous occupant or something left by him because he couldn't pack it—and I began to eat those pastries and to enjoy them. But the day before I was to fly from Belgrade back to Paris I remembered Chopin's walking stick, and this is what had happened: I had not brought it from room 321 to 307, so I asked the friendly man at the desk to see if the stick was still in 321. It was not. The man said, Two Italians are in there. And that was the end of the Chopin walking stick. And it is the end of this memoir of my visit to Warsaw and my death there, if you like, or anybody's death there, or anywhere else. That is what it comes to, and I feel it is enough, although it is really so little as to be really nothing, man, nothing at all, so you went to Warsaw in your 72nd year and with you went your disease and your pal Old Red Tail and your life, your entire life so far, going on and on but scheduled to stop.

TALES FROM THE VIENNA STREETS

A Play in Eighteen Scenes

Vienna's English Theatre

1080 Wien, Josefsgasse 12, Telefon 42 12 60

World Premiere
Play Things
by
William Saroyan

"TRIUMPHAL ENTRY OF HELIOS", CEILING FRESCO IN VIENNA'S ENGLISH THEATRE

Cover of Theater Program from the world premiere of William Saroyan's "Play Things," produced by Vienna's English Theatre on June 29, 1980.

WORLD PREMIERE

PLAY THINGS

a theatrical lark
by
WILLIAM SAROYAN

as concieved and directed by
MAI ZETTERLING

with illustrations from
ANDY WARHOL

(art © 1980 by Andy Warhol)

ONE THING AND ANOTHER
cast
(in order of appearance)

The One Woman Philharmonic . . . . CAROLINE JOHN
The Little Man . . . . PETER O'FARRELL
Mime . . . . LOZ NEWEY
Mime . . . . SARA VAN BEERS
The Fat Man . . . . THICK WILSON
The Thin Man . . . . FELIX RICE
The Tall Lady . . . . DANA GILLESPIE
The Fat Lady . . . . OLWEN GRIFFITHS

PRODUCED BY FRANZ SCHAFRANEK

Set Construction by
WOLFGANG MÜLLER KARBACH

under the supervision of
TAMARE

Musical Collation and Original Composition by
MICHAEL HURD

Costume Designs executed by
LIZ DA COSTA

with the assistance of
SARA GREEN

Company Stage Manager . . . . JAMES GILL
Production Co-Ordinator . . . . ALAN LEVY
Resident Stage Manager . . . . MARTIN LAWTON
Assistant Stage Managers . . . . EVA WANIECZEK
                                              AHMED SBAI
Sound . . . . JUPITER (London)
Lighting . . . . ERNST BRAUN
                                              HELMUT NORIZ
Hair Styles . . . . BURGI
Casting . . . . ROLF KRUGER (London)
Sound Technician . . . . GEOFFREY EALES

The cast list and production staff of the premiere of "Play Things" by William
Saroyan from the official program.

The cast of "Play Things" on stage after the premiere performance at Vienna's English Theatre, June 29, 1980. (Photo Franz Schafranek)

William Saroyan at the premiere of "Play Things" at Vienna's English Theatre, June 29, 1980. Next to Saroyan from right to left are Ruth Brinkmann, co-founder of Vienna's English Theatre; Director Mai Zetterling; Austrian Ambassador to the United Nations, Dr. Fischer and his wife; and American Ambassador Reiser and his wife. (Photo Franz Schafranek)

Franz Schafranek co-founder and Director of Vienna's English Theatre. (Photo by "picture born," Vienna)

William Saroyan 74 Rue Taitbout 75009 Paris Thursday July 17 1980 1:30 P.M.
Tales From the Vienna Streets, a play, ~~ballet, opera, etcetera etcetera.~~
    1. The one scene is the entrance to and part of the brandnew Coffee
House called Hayakor, on Graben, or The Ditch, not far from St. Stephens,
where the old man who is sometimes called The Lark is working his fingers
vibrato upon the keys of his music-box and chanting falsetto something that
sounds like homage to forgotten truth and places and people, and longing
for the angels and light of the last place, so to put it. There is an
easy indifference among the people in the Hayakor to the tensions of reality
itself and the enjoyment of art, including the falsetto chant, although
now and then one of the people at one of the four tiny round-top tables
puts down his paper or book to put his head sideways in order to listen *and*
a little more earnestly. *Hayek, Gabrione?*   *Alec* *children,*
    Van, ~~White:~~ ~~Alec Aroon?~~ (:Puts down cup of coffee.)   *now*
    Schmidt: Al*ec*? ~~Alexander?~~ Aroon? Wh*at* is Aroon?   *and*
    Van: *A* name. Are you Alec Aroon?   *forever,*
    Schmidt: Oh, no, Sigmund Freud.
    Van: I am ~~a waiter at~~ the Hayakor Coffee House, ~~this place,~~ *My* name
is Van. What do you do, Herr Frog?
    Schmidt: Freud, ~~Freud,~~ not Frog, Sigmund Freud, I am an expert in
dreams. I would have been only a writer except that there is really less
and less fame in it, and not very much money, either.
    Van: An expert in dreams, ~~did you say?~~ How? Why? Who remembers dreams?
    Schmidt: I do, you do, but women especially do. The dreams of troubled
women tell us the truth about men and women ~~long ago.~~ Women really dream.
    Van: Like that one over there? Don't turn quickly, she'll know we're
talking about her. Desdemona, Cleopatra, St. Joan, Mata Hari, Florence
Nightingale, and let me see who she said she was this morning when she
came in and sat down. Oh yes, Lily of the Valley.
    Alice: Not Lily of the Valley, ~~you fool.~~ Lily of Laguna. Laguna,
Laguna, do you understand? Spanish for lagoon. A body of water. A
mulatto, as I am, entirely imaginary, the darling of the English song-writer
Leslie Stuart who went to Alabama and found her waiting, ~~for him~~ and wrote
his best song. Have you no sense of history, at all? Do you concern yourself
only ~~with~~ fame and fortune? Of course, of course, how silly of me, you are
~~a waiter at~~ the Hayakor Coffee House. Well, then, bring me another coffee,
please, and when you set the cup down I'll lean forward so that you can look
down into my bodice. ~~Why~~ do you do that?   *onorand*
    Van: Why do you ~~think~~ I do that? I do not do that. I am a waiter.
I set down a small cup of coffee on a small saucer in a proper place on
the small table. One coffee, please. (Voice: Ho.) Why do you announce *a*
~~your~~ character ~~for the day~~ every time you come in and sit down? Are you
an actress, ~~perhaps?~~ A*re* you ~~are~~ waiting to be called by Shakespear*e or*
Moliere, or Lope de Vega? (The chanting stops.)
    Schmidt: Lope de Vega? You know about such people as Lope de Vega?
    Alice: Something's changed. What is it that's changed? Something's
different. I have got to get things straight. Something just happened.
What was it? Is there nobody else in Vienna who wants to understand everything
    Van: The Lark just stopped singing, that's all, Madame.
    Alice: Don't Madame me, whoever you are. Why has he stopped? I don't
want him to stop. This is not Vienna if he is not singing. St. Stephens
is not St. Stephens. Restored, to be sure---after the carnage of the
battle of the monsters. Graben is not Graben, the Ditch is not the Ditch.
You are not you, and I am not Lily of Laguna if the Lark stops singing.
Sing again, ~~sing again,~~ please. I command ~~that~~ you*r* sing again. (The
Lark begins a new chant.) I thank you, and I shall be kind to you with *Esther*
all of myself, as you see fit, if you dare. Oh, and this song is even *better*
~~more angelic~~ than the other. More human, also. We do not really need to
be ashamed of being human, although it would be preposterous if we took
pride in it. We have been taking pride in it since we learned to talk.
It's about time we tried not talking ~~for a century or two.~~ Think of it,
everybody going about his business in total silence---just looking, just
smelling, just touching./.
    Van: Here is your coffee, Madame. Oh, forgive me. Lily of Laguna.

The first page and first scene of Saroyan's original typescript of *Tales from the Vienna Streets* edited by the author for the Vienna's English Theatre production which never took place. (Photo Dickran Kouymjian)

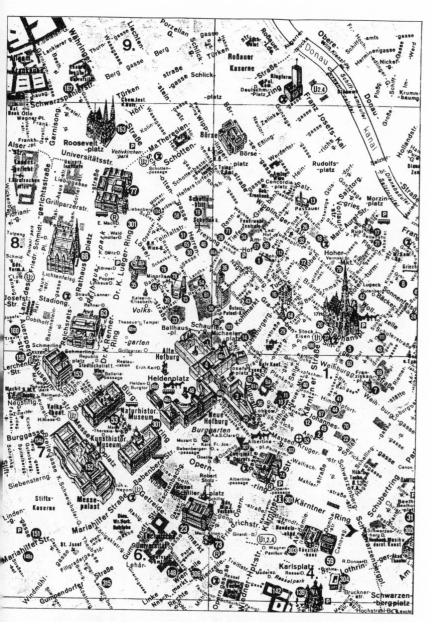

Tourist map of central Vienna in 1980. The sites mentioned in *Tales from the Vienna Streets:* 1. St. Stephan's Cathedral in the center right, 2. the Graben to its left between numbers 16, 64 and 29, 3. the Armenian Mekhitarist Monastery ("Mechit K." with a cross) below number 158 to the far left.

During the writing of Tales, Saroyan continued to draw and paint almost every afternoon, either on recycled paper or in used books that he bought from one of the many dealers in his neighborhood. The lower part of this double painting was done on July 21, 1980 when he was halfway finished with Tales and the upper, the day after he finished the play, July 26. On July 20 he even dedicated a simple drawing ''For the play Tales from the Vienna Streets.'' (Photo Dickran Kouymjian)

An early painting of Mekhitar of Sebastia (1676-1749), founder and first Abbot of the Mekhitarist Brotherhood.

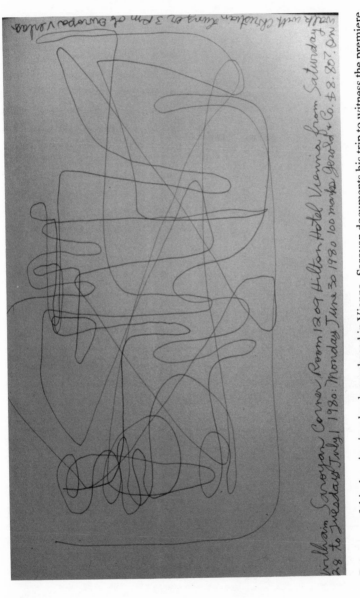

William Saroyan Corner Room 1209 Hilton Hotel Vienna from Saturday (June) 28 to Tuesday July 1 1980: Monday June 30 1980 100 marks Gerold & Co. $8.80? On walk with Christian Lunzer at 3 pm at Europa Verlag

By means of this drawing in a book purchased in Vienna, Saroyan documents his trip to witness the premiere of "Play Things." "William Saroyan Corner room 1209 Hilton Hotel Vienna from Saturday (June) 28 to Tuesday July 1 1980: Monday June 30 1980 100 marks Gerola & Co. $8.80? On walk with Christian Lunzer 3 pm of Europa Verlag." (Photo Dickran Kouymjian)

THE PEOPLE

VAN VASPOURAGANIAN, *owner of the Haydakor Coffee House*

HO, *for* HOVAKIM, *the Armenian rendering of the Biblical Joachim, Bitlistzi [from Bitlis],* [VAN'S] *first cousin, his mother was the sister of* VAN'S *father.*

SCHMIDT, *a variety of men at a table in a Coffee House, all civilized, anywhere from 44 to 68 or so.*

ALICE, *a variety of women, but like* SCHMIDT *always also the one person. Each has a slight costume change in the interval after each of the scenes, and in the last scene, 18, is clearly and memorably the same as in Scene 1.*

GIRL, *the very daughter of the human race, the girl of the world, she can be any girl, all girls, and do anything: dance ballet, as she does; or walk the streets; or become the mother who is forever sought by the father and sought by their unborn— carrying on the tradition of continuity, at any rate.* ANNA?

BOY, *a son of the human race, but apparently with dominant female reality, and aspirations for motherhood instead of fatherhood.* ALFIE.

GUARDEN OFFIZIER

FIVE MEN, TWO WOMEN, *unless I have forgotten somebody, and in any case* THE LARK *or somebody else might materialize in the play.*

THE PLACE

Vienna, the Haydakor Coffee House just off Graben, or The Ditch, not far from St. Stephens.

THE TIME

A summer day in 1980.

NOTE: The play was written in one act with eighteen scenes in Paris between July 17 and 24, 1980. The detailed descriptions of the characters and the stage directions for each scene are Saroyan's.

SCENE 1

The single setting is the brand new Haydakor Coffee House on Graben, or The Ditch, not far from St. Stephens, where the old man who is sometimes called THE LARK, *unseen, is working his fingers vibrato upon the keys of his music-box and chanting falsetto something that sounds like homage to forgotten truth and places and people, and longing for the angels and light of the last place, so to put it. There is an easy indifference among the people in the Haydakor to the tensions of reality itself and the enjoyment of art, including the falsetto chant, although now and then one of the people at one of the four tiny round-top tables puts down his paper or book to put his head sideways in order to listen a little more.*

Two tiny round-top tables at which two dummies sit, each with a removable head, for variety from one scene to another. One table with handbag on newspaper, at which ALICE *sits. A table, across the room, with book, pad and pencil, at which* SCHMIDT *sits. Nobody smokes cigarettes, cigars, or pipes. The coffee cups are bright red, the saucers dark black. Two other tables, for* ALFIE *and the* GIRL, *first at one table, then each at a separate table. The tables are painted bright chalk white. The dropcurtain is a large painting of various parts of Vienna brought together into something like a work of art.*

VAN
Hayek, Bahrone? *(Puts down cup of coffee)*

SCHMIDT
Alec? Aroon? Who is Alec Aroon?

VAN
Is that a name? Are *you* Alec Aroon?

SCHMIDT
Oh, no, Sigmund Freud.

VAN

I am the owner of the Haydakor Coffee House, this place. My name is Van. What do you do, Herr Frog?

SCHMIDT

Freud, not Frog, *Sigmund* Freud, I am an expert in dreams. I would have been only a writer except that there is really less and less fame in it, and not very much money, either.

VAN

An expert in dreams? How? Why? Who remembers dreams?

SCHMIDT

I do, you do, but women *especially* do. The dreams of troubled women tell us the truth about men and women and children, now and forever. Women *really* dream.

VAN

Like that one over there? Don't turn quickly, she'll know we're talking about her. Desdemona, Cleopatra, St. Joan, Mata Hari, Florence Nightingale, and let me see who she said she was this morning when she came in and sat down. Oh yes, Lily of the Valley.

ALICE

Not Lily of the *Valley,* Sir. Lily of *Laguna.* Laguna, Laguna, do you understand? Spanish for lagoon. A body of water. A mulatto, as I am, entirely imaginary, the darling of the English song-writer Leslie Stuart who went to Alabama and found her waiting and wrote his best song. Have you no sense of history at all? Do you concern yourself only with fame and fortune? Of course, of course, how silly of me, you are the owner of the Haydakor Coffee House. Well, then, bring me another coffee, please, and when you set the cup down I'll lean forward so that you can look down into my bodice. Why do you do that?

VAN

Why do you believe I do that? I do *not* do that. I am owner
and waiter. I set down a small cup of coffee on a small saucer
in a proper place on the small table. *One coffee, please!*

VOICE

Ho.

VAN

Why do you announce a new character every time you come
in and sit down? Are you an actress? Are you waiting to be
called by Shakespeare or Moliere, or Lope de Vega? *(The
chanting stops)*

SCHMIDT

Lope de Vega? You know about such people as Lope de Vega?

ALICE

Something's changed. What is it that's changed? Something's
different. I have got to get things straight. Something just
happened. What was it? Is there nobody else in Vienna who
wants to understand everything?

VAN

The Lark just stopped singing, that's all, Madame.

ALICE

Don't Madame me, whoever you are. *Why* has he stopped? I
don't want him to stop. This is not Vienna if he is not singing.
St. Stephens is not St. Stephens. *Restored,* to be sure—after
the carnage of the battle of the monsters. Graben is not Graben,
the Ditch is not the Ditch. You are not you and I am not Lily
of Laguna if the Lark stops singing. Sing again, please. I
command you to sing again. (THE LARK *begins a new chant*) I
thank you, and I shall be kind to you with all of myself, as you
see fit, if you dare. Oh, and *this* song is even better than the
other. More human. We do not really need to be ashamed of

159

being human, although it would be preposterous if we took pride
in it. We have been taking pride in it since we learned to talk.
It's about time we tried *not* talking. Think of it, everybody going
about his business in total silence—just looking, just smelling,
just touching.

VAN

Here is your coffee, Madame. Oh, forgive me. Lily of Laguna.

ALICE

Thank you. You may put your hand anywhere you like.

VAN

Here, on top of your head, then. (*To* SCHMIDT) Hayek,
Bahrone?

SCHMIDT

Ah, no. Franz Schubert fast asleep in the granite of the statue
in the Park, poor boy, with syphilis, and no money at all.

SCENE 2

*Perhaps the statue of Schubert in the Park is seen on the screen,
and a very familiar piece of his music is heard, such as
"Traumerei," to which* ALICE *moves as in dream-dance, while*
SCHMIDT *holds his face high as if remembering or trying to think,
while* VAN *moves among the tables at which dummy men and
women sit, removing cups and saucers.*

*A young man comes in cautiously, chooses a table, sits, and waves
to the door, whereupon a young woman comes in, looks around,
and goes and sits at the table. They look at one another while*
ALICE *dances slowly around the table. The Schubert fades away,
and is followed first by silence, and then by special tinkling music
composed by an appropriate composer, perhaps Loris
Tjeknavorian: music as if made by plates permitted to gently fall*

upon a marble-top table, as in vaudeville of Germany about a
hundred years ago, along the lines of "Oh, Tannenbaum,*" or*
"Silent Night." Slowly, steadily a dream scene gives way to reality,
or at any rate coffee-house reality.

SCHMIDT

Who? I mean, who did you say? Beethoven? Was that the name
you said? Well, not that it really matters all that much, but I
believe I can tell you this about Beethoven—he was not anything
at all like your typical Viennese. I didn't know him. At least
I didn't know him well, but Beethoven for a number of very
important years of his life lived in our neighborhood, and now
and then as a dog I saw him finding his way to a bone. He was
very facial, there was much face to Beethoven. But behind the
face was all that activity, you know. *Music,* but almost insane—
but perhaps you prefer the music by the other Viennese Ludwigs.

VAN

Who? Me? Well, the truth is I don't understand the part about
the dog. I mean, if you really want to know, I don't know who
the dog is. At first I thought it was yourself, and since you are
not a dog I presumed you meant dog as certain writers do, as
when jolly young men speak to one another about jolly young
women and say *you dog you.* And then I thought you were
speaking of Beethoven, but not the man, you were speaking
of Beethoven the dog, and I felt sure you had something in mind
in this transformation that perhaps you would not be unwilling
to explain. My work is simple, as we see, but God knows how
swiftly I suspect all manner of complicated things, almost
without question, and perhaps that is the secret of the success
of the Haydakor Coffee House, only a short time on the Graben.
People who come here suspect that anything they say or think
or dream or remember, or *forget,* even, is not beyond my
understanding. Were *you* the dog in that Vienna neighborhood,
or was it Beethoven?

SCHMIDT

I believe the Lovers would like a coffee. Please inform them that if they will not be offended let it be with my compliments, and put a little brandy in each cup, if they like the idea. Ideas mean so much, you might say, to each of us while we are young, although of course we really never stop being young. The muscles settle down, that's all.

VAN

The gentleman would like to offer you coffee, is that all right? In other words, no charge. He also offers to have a drop of brandy poured into each cup, if you like. No charge. Is that all right? (*The* BOY *looks at the* GIRL, *and they both nod to* VAN, *and then to* SCHMIDT) Two coffees, with brandy.

VOICE

Ho.

SCHMIDT

Who is it ho-ing back there? I mean, there's a special quality to the ho we hear out here. It isn't exactly what anybody might expect in Vienna. I have the feeling that it is part of a lost song of some kind, from far away. Mongolia, perhaps, where the horses are all ponies and the riders are all Mongols and very dignified out there in the vast steppes. Great good God Almighty, how I would like to die in Mongolia astride my own pony far out in the vast steppes.

VAN

What are your symptoms?

SCHMIDT

I never kept track. *All* of them, I suppose. All, all, all of them. You name it, I have it. Don't you? And you, young man? Don't you? Is there ever any of us who is free of the symptoms of mortality? If you breathe, you are flawed. But let us not make too much of it, for if you breathe you are also flawless.

SCENE 3

There is now a ballet in which breathing, inhale and exhale, ebb and flow, high tide and low tide, intermingle with touches of music by first Schubert, then Beethoven, then Strauss, any of the famous waltzes, and finally by the composer of the score for this work: "Tales from the Vienna Woods," "The Blue Danube," "The Dragonfly," "Barcarole." And from the Street the sudden participation of THE LARK. *The* LOVERS *do an amateur pas de deux.* ALICE *invites* SCHMIDT *to dance, but he brings out his wallet and gives her a piece of currency which she folds and puts into her bodice. Quietude.* VAN *sets two coffees on the table for the* BOY *and* GIRL.

VAN

Are you dancers, then? Stars of ballet?

BOY

Oh, no, no, no. Nothing like that. Oh, wouldn't it be really exciting if we were?

GIRL

But we are, we are, but only when we can't help ourselves. We will never dance again like *that*. Will we? Will we?

BOY

Oh, yes we will, yes we will. Look here, childbirth does not mean the end of everything. We *will* dance.

GIRL

Oh, we will, won't we?

SCHMIDT

Now, look here, enough is enough. It is not necessary for you to speak cheap thought in the cheap writing of a cheap multimillionaire novelist living in a mansion on the outskirts of Hollywood, once inhabited by Theda Bara, then by Rudolph

Valentino. Will we, will we, won't we, won't we? So you're pregnant, so enjoy it and let the multi-millionaire turn his silly talent to the procreative procedures of silent mothers—and fathers...to be. What would he have them say, pray tell? Shall we, will we, can we, ought we, do we, don't we—and by that time everything tumbles out by the billions and everything moves along the same as ever.

GIRL

I'm afraid, I'm fragile, I feel funny, it isn't fair. He does what he does, and I let him, I want him to, but then things start happening to me and nothing like that happens to him, and it's not fair, that's all. Is it?

ALICE

It is, for you are never *altogether* helpless about any of it, are you? If you like, right now, you can get up and leave him sitting there with his coffee unfinished and you can go to somebody for your choice of action. Or you can sit and sip with him and think about everything—and believe, and wait, and let it happen, and after it happens you can believe that this one, by God, this sweet infant girl, she is the one at last, or this strong infant boy, he is the one at last, and his father did it, and his mother did it, and boy or girl each of them has all these amazing parts, these incredibly perfect fingers and toes, eyes, ears, arms, legs, lips, genitals, do you want to believe it isn't fair that you help in this nonsense, this folly, this arrogance, this humility? You can't ask *him* to do it, he hasn't got the apparatus for it. What do you have to do? You only have to wait. Is waiting all that much trouble?

GIRL

I'm afraid. Deep down in my bones I think something will happen. I'll die. I won't dance, I'll die. And he won't. And we love one another as if loving we were no longer each of us the secret we know and never know, we are something new, together. So where am I when I die, and where is he?

BOY

I won't have it. I know a surgeon, it's very safe, you won't feel rotten afterwards, I won't have you terrified this way. Come on, we'll go to the surgeon. I have the money. *Cash.* Right here. Saved.

GIRL

You dog. You saved money for an abortion, for me? A violence on my body? A murder? The destruction of nature? How dare you? Really, how dare you save money for an abortion and not one penny for a black negligee?

BOY

I just don't want you to die, that's all.

GIRL

But what about nature? What about whoever I'm pregnant with? The girl made out of light, the boy made out of laughter? All I am feeling is that—somehow, somehow, and I don't quite know how—it's not fair, that's all. I want you. I want myself. I want us. I want the girl of light, the boy of laughter. I don't know why, but I do, I want them, and I am terrified of the power of this wanting. I am fragile.

BOY

I am too, perhaps even more than you. Have it, and if you die, I'll kill myself. I swear it. Because I know you won't die, but will he be the boy of laughter?

SCENE 4

Music and dance interval

SCHMIDT

I gather, it comes to me in a manner of speaking, I tend to notice such things, it is not exactly a gift, it is rather the opposite of a gift, a taking away, but whatever it is, let me remark, if you don't mind, that I gather this, which I feel I must make known.

ALICE

Are you talking to me?

BOY

No, I believe he's talking to *me*. Am I right, and did I thank you for the coffee, or in my rapture, did I forget?

GIRL

Your rapture? What about my rapture? Which I am sure you *somewhat* suspect? How terrible it is for me to be so fragile as to feel both rapture and terror, but it is the truth, I am absolutely in a panic about this thing. Why did we do it? Surely he is talking to *me,* is that so, sir, whoever you are?

SCHMIDT

Well, yes, and then again no, not really. What can I say in a casual conversation in a coffee house, in a little coffee-time idle chitchat? What can I say to you that is not being said to you by everybody and everything all the time in the only language that has any meaning? I refer to your joining of the human *procedure.* I refer to becoming a living party of the first part. I refer to being part of the *continuation.* I refer to the fact that you are at this moment a living demonstration of how mystery itself makes all of the true decisions and by that means keeps us all in place, give or take who each of us turns out to be or learns how to become. You are nature itself, indeed the whole universe with its endless solar systems growing in your belly, so what could I possibly say to you that could mean anything at all? I am hushed by the hush of your connection to the reality of the happening in your belly, by the way you are still able to dance, and to dispute with your husband about who is who and what is what.

GIRL

He's not my husband, but let's not make a big deal out of that, he is certainly the man I did not drive off. I certainly took part in the game, so all the things you said may turn out to be untrue, after all, is that not so?

SCHMIDT

Please do not discourage me from the habit of believing that the things I say mean *something*. I have lived with that belief and I have witnessed a confirmation of the theory now and then, but I must confess not too often. If he is not your husband, why *isn't* he? Is it because he is the husband of somebody else?

ALICE

Or might it be slightly more accurate to say the wife? I know such men, and I'm rather fond of them as of course so is the dear child manufacturing herself and a smidgen of *himself* inside her belly for all of us to behold with incurable curiosity and even something like happiness. Of course she is fond of him, but not the way I am. She is fond of him as a man, and I as an amusing protest of nature itself against the rigidity of itself, nature quarreling with nature and all of it in the form of funny sayings, tones of voice, and gossip. He knows pretty much everything about everybody, now, don't you, dear boy?

BOY

What nonsense. What's going on here? This is silly. Why did you insist that we must come here to the Haydakor Coffee House instead of any one of a dozen others? Do you know these people? Are they members of your family? Have you brought me here to embarrass me? What is this place, the Last Stop? Are we all dreaming, or are we being dreamed? Waiter, I insist on paying for my own coffee, although I cannot afford to pay for the brandy, which wasn't my idea in the first place. Kindly present me with the tab and I'll pay and go.

VAN

Everything is paid, but if you would like another coffee I will be glad to call out as I do, One coffee.

VOICE

Ho.

BOY

No thanks, I do not want another coffee.

VAN

Cancel one coffee.

VOICE

Ho.

BOY

This is where I came in, this is where I go out.

GIRL

What's the matter with you? *(He goes)* Wait for me.

ALICE

Let him go, he has a husband somewhere, and they want a child, so they got the idea that they might use you and become the father and mother of their own dear child—two men. Relax, what's done is done, sit back, let the natural procedure have its way, for it is going to do so in any case. Am I right about him?

GIRL

Well.

ALICE

It's all right, he's a dear boy, do not go berserk in your soul.

SCENE 5

From far away a voice that might be Richard Tauber's sings "Dein ist Mein Ganzes Herz." HO, as a very large dog with a face that resembles Beethoven's walks from the kitchen among the tables, and nobody pays much attention to him. He stands up, removes the mask, looks at it, puts it back on, gets down on his hands and knees and goes back into the kitchen. A soprano sings "Golden Days" by Franz Lehar or somebody, even though in The Student Prince it is always a tenor who sings that song. When she comes to "how we laughed," she stops. There is silence, and she breaks into tears, but it turns out to be the Girl crying softly.

SCHMIDT

Who was that that came out of the kitchen?

VAN

Ho. My cousin Hovakim. He does that kind of thing now and then. It helps the hours go by.

SCHMIDT

I thought it was Beethoven. I mean the very special—now, what do I mean? Grandeur is what we think about when we think about Beethoven, so what is the very special thing about Beethoven as a big dog that I seem to feel?

VAN

Well, whatever it is, it is nothing, isn't that right?

SCHMIDT

Well, yes, most likely, but it *could* be something, could it not.

VAN

How, pray tell? Now, forgive me, is anybody here praying? I mean, I do not use the phrase pray tell, and yet I seem to be using it quite a lot. Who's praying in the Haydakor Coffee House?

GIRL

I am of course. Oh, Father, send him back to me, to be the father of the one I shall present to you as the only gift I can offer. Send him back. I will sit here forever waiting for him, Father.

VAN

We close at midnight, but there is a cot in a small room in the back that you are welcome to during the dark hours of shutness, emptiness, loss, and longing. I mean, I won't put you out, not *enceinte,* if that's the word. But *are* you *enceinte,* are you with child, for I have heard that there are false pregnancies quite frequently, not excluding a swelling of the belly which turns out to be gas and takes the course of escaping gas when everybody expects a child to be born unto us, how does that go? For unto us a child is born? Big deal, so it happens a hundred thousand times a day, or maybe these days even more, and nobody says, For unto us a child is born. It happens, that's all, and somebody comes out of that perfect place and ah well, cries and cries, half with joy, half with despair most likely. We close at midnight, but have no care, you will not be put out. I am the owner, the room is mine, and you are welcome to it—while you wait, if you **are** *enceinte*—is that really the word? It sounds as if it is, but there are others, like knocked-up, rather vulgar in a way, no offense, child, it may be that you are *not* knocked-up, but whatever, whatever, you will not be sent out into the streets of Vienna to find your way nowhere. You can have the little room and the little cot. I changed the bedding this morning. You are welcome to it.

GIRL

I couldn't take your bed, but thank you, but thank you, but thank you, but now worse than ever the fragility frightens me—I'll gladly give God the gift, and then die, but who cares about that when it comes to giving God the gift? How differently every life must be than what the gift somehow believed it *would* be.

ALICE

And how differently also every death. I wanted mine to be so
right, and when it happened it was so wrong I had to laugh,
nothing could possibly have been more wrong than my death,
it was a musical hall joke, that's what it was. Lights, I screamed,
I'm over here in the dark, for God's sake, put a spot on me,
please, this is no way to die.

SCHMIDT

When was that? I don't doubt that you died, but when did it
happen? I mean, I am here to learn. We are here to learn. They
are here to learn. She is here to learn. He was here to learn,
and having done so, went off—who was the English poet who
said something like "gliding like a Queen." Did you notice
that about his going?

ALICE

Oh yes, oh yes. And when he goes to drag, he makes natural
women who *are* able to get knocked-up or to become *enceinte*
or with child, he makes them feel ashamed to be who they are,
for he is so much more artfully female than they could ever
be. If he comes back, I almost wish he comes back in drag—
but if he does, dear child, just remember that the one thing he
can't do is get knocked-up, no matter what, if you know what
I mean. So far, so far nature does not allow it, that's all.

SCHMIDT

It boggles the mind, almost.

GIRL

How cruel you are.

SCENE 6

VOICE

Beethoven's Fifth, ladies and gentlemen, at its most famous opening phrase, followed by a dozen or more variations by the composer for this theatrical work, Loris Tjeknavorian, who came to Vienna from Tehran thirty years ago as a boy of ten, to study with the Mekhitarist monks at their famous Roman Catholic Monastery—theology, German history and literature, composition, including counterpoint, and to read and write and speak the Armenian language. Look at him go, folks. The kid's a genius, no less, and so are you, each of you, folks, so share with one another the good luck of it. If it weren't for genius, how terrible it would be to be a human being.

GIRL

I beg to disagree. Nobody is a genius except a genius, but everybody of the female gender, as well as many of the male gender, *hope* that they may somehow present to God, to Heaven, to the World, and to the human family a genius. Otherwise, why would everybody keep trying, why would every woman in the world suffer herself to become *enceinte,* or regret not having done so, regret, and regret, all her life? To have come and to go without giving the gift. All the same I am fragile and afraid, there is no reason for me to pretend that I am not terrified— what shall I do when I die?

ALICE

Look here, you are not going to die. Indeed, no matter how fragile and frightened you are, you will have no real or special trouble presenting us with the gift and we shall all of us thank you and be proud of your strong character, to thrust aside both fragility and fear in that famous ancient contract of women with God. And as the man says, perhaps you are not *enceinte,* perhaps it is gas, and if that is so permit me to ask, would you feel glad, would you feel relieved and let the gas go in its traditional manner, or would you feel terrible, cheated out of your birthright—no pun, but there it is, a woman does have a birthright, the right to give birth, and a man does not. Would you feel humiliated, freakish, silly, fraudulent, or what?—Well, think about it, that's all right, but when you learn the answer please pass it along. If it is something you don't want everybody to hear, come and whisper it to me, I will not betray you. The truth is the truth, but of course that is only a saying, and the truth is really never the truth, and the untruth is really never the untruth, each is moving, and you need not concern yourself too much with how and why and to where truth and untruth are moving. Will you rejoice that you are empty of the connection with the big parade, so to call it. Or will you fall into such profound regret that you will be speechless for the rest of your life—except for the saying of all of the things of gossip that everybody quickly settles down to saying and living by. Take your time, think about it, it is our story, you see—not just you and I, because we are female, but all of us, for how much real difference is there between male and female except that the male cannot become *enceinte,* for we are all come from male and female together, and something of each side enters into each of us during the condition of being connected to all of nature—animal, plant, mineral, water, fire, air, and mystery all entangled together. Will you be delighted to be delivered of the fraudulence of your own private connection with the public connection and go dancing out of here back to the easy fun of butterflies flapping about lightly from flower to flower, or will you feel loss so great as to hush you forever because nature tricked you, God tricked you, man tricked you?

GIRL

I'll kill myself if I'm not pregnant. Does that answer your question? I don't care if he is a Queen. He got me *enceinte,* as all of you keep saying. And I don't care if it was to provide himself and *his* husband, or lover, or whatever it is, to provide him with the child they both want so desperately, or believe they do. He himself told me that Jean Cocteau, whoever he is, oh, I know, a French writer, told everybody that the tragedy of his life was that he could not get pregnant. And there have been many others, perhaps each of them, including the one who seems to be my husband, although he told me that it isn't quite that simple, the husband is also all the time the wife, and vice versa. Didn't the famous old man of German letters say there are more things under the sun than mice and men might ever know? I would kill myself. I would find out how. My condition is more to me than anything in the human story, possible or impossible, and I am still just as fragile and frightened as ever. *I want my gift.*

ALICE

You may have it, then. And we in turn shall wait with you and watch and think about who it is to be and if there is to be genius in his brain, and grace in his flawless little fingers and toes, and parts. Or hers.

GIRL

His. I want a son. Don't ask me why, but I do.

SCENE 7

During the preceding interval of opera, ballet, tableau, or whatever, as perhaps each of the earlier ones, SCHMIDT *has got up for a change of costume and character, nothing more than a coat or cape, hat or walking stick, something more haberdashic than profound. The same sort of thing has happened to* ALICE. SCHMIDT, *the father of the human race, so to put it, then* ALICE, the mother. But each might just be the Step-Father and the Step-*Mother, too. Their leaving of their places to make these superficial changes are to be noticed, and* VAN *is to go to them each time as if to confirm the old customer, or to be at the service of the new one.*

VAN

Don't I know you from somewhere? Hayek, Bahrone?

SCHMIDT

Franz Lehar, if you don't mind.

VAN

Wasn't there a Franz Liszt?

SCHMIDT

There was, and there is. Franz is a very popular name, as we see, but it means nothing more than boy, then man, son, then father, if Heaven permits or compels. And this Alec Aroon, he is your father, is he not? Don't tell me, please, the question is for fun, it is rhetorical, we all like a bit of fun now and then, you know. Franz Lehar, at your service.

VAN

I don't want you to be at my service, in the Haydakor Coffee House I am the one who is at your service, with Ho helping out in the kitchen, and I think you will agree that his help is excellent as you take the first sip of this coffee.

SCHMIDT

Ho is ho, and ha is ha, and if ho is in the kitchen, and ha is in the Ditch, who is who and how is how, not what, not when, not where, and all of the other who's and how's we live by. In Vienna, in Vienna, a little of which we have settled dead center in the heart of all of the great cities of the world: Paris, Berlin, Moscow, Rome, Madrid, London, New York, San Francisco. When I think of what we have done for the human race, I say, Sir, without fear of successful contradiction, repudiation, or vanity, I am—proud. That's the very word, although somehow it is not quite enough. I am astonished. How we kept the Danube rolling and rolling like blood in the veins of the entire living human race. And then our lights and costumings and voices and songs and dances and that magical spirit hovering over everything forever, almost, just beyond all the glitter and melody and dance and turning and turning and hoping and dreaming and being fulfilled, being fulfilled, being totally fulfilled, not being frustrated, not being denied, everything longed for received and achieved, but without a horrible struggle, without death everywhere, dead bodies everywhere, sour mouths everywhere, diseased genitals everywhere, broken hearts everywhere, broken heads, broken minds, shattered nerves, insanity, hysteria, pain, astonishment, disbelief, and then more pain, blood all over everything, in the face of God splattered with blood. When I think of all that do you imagine for an instant, son of Alexander Aroon, I presume, when I think of what it has been the privilege of Vienna to do for the rest of the great cities of the world and for the rest of the human family, I ask myself and all Viennese, What happened? Why were we chosen to do so much for so many so pleasantly, so lightly, in two-four time, in two-two time, in waltz time, in living time? Is it possible, then, that it *is* true, that it *is* in the blood, that all blood is blood, but there is simply no getting away from the simple truth that Vienna blood is not Peking blood or Tierra del Fuego blood or Cairo or Constantinople or Boston, and we all know, do we not, that Boston blood is beautiful blood, it is almost Godly blood, but even so it is different, it is not as unaccountable as Vienna blood. Great good God Almighty—and I *am* praying—how we laughed, how we danced, how we turned and turned, kissed and kissed, and enjoyed, enjoyed ourselves, enjoyed eternity in bed with us, and then went to Sacher's for the famous chocolate cake, sitting and stirring the small spoon in the cup of the lovely coffee, looking into the eyes of one another, and rejoicing in Vienna, Vienna. What shall I say? How shall I put it? I am at a loss for words.

VAN

Au contraire, Sir, and good customer. It is I who am at a loss for words. But I can say this, I believe. I wish, I deeply wish that the music and life you speak of had been a little less heavy with sorrow, a little less aware of the emptiness and tragedy of human life, I wish it had been just a little more, how shall I say it, innocent? Yes, *innocent.* Unaware. Why didn't you *really* laugh? And *dance?* And all the rest of that coffee-and-Sacher-chocolate-cake desperation, pretense, and failure?

SCENE 8

During this interval of song, dance, tableau, parade, mime, acrobatics, Olympic athletic events like weight-lifting until the world itself is hoisted overhead by somebody, during whatever constitutes this interval the voice of THE LARK *out on the Graben, or the Ditch, comes so close as to be impossible not to listen to very carefully. And then as if from an old phonograph, and an early record is heard the voice of somebody like the famous singer Maria Jeritza, meanwhile* ALICE *coming back to her place, this time as a rather special street-walker, not showy at all, but somehow clearly available for special transactions involving half an hour or half a century if that makes sense and somebody can pick up the tab.*

VAN

Like I say, haven't I met you somewhere before—I hope.

ALICE

Yes, we've met, I'm sure of it, I certainly feel that I have met everybody, and the few I haven't met have seen me from afar, for I am a member of the profession.

VAN

What profession is that?

ALICE

A member in good standing furthermore. The profession of acting, of course. I am of the theatre.

VAN

What plays have I seen you in? I mean, if there is a big hit not too far from here I sometimes find the time to get there and to see at least some of the play. I can't see all of a play, because

177

they take too long, and the best part seems to be later on, the part that satisfies expectations aroused in the earlier part. I may have seen you on the boards in a play somewhere, or two plays, or three—there's only one play of course.

ALICE

And what play is *that?*

VAN

Why the play here, right here, yourself at this tiny table receiving your cup of coffee from me, also right here, and passing the time of day, or night, in very simple idle words of questions and answers with nobody charged with any crime. The play of *being,* the play that starts and stops every minute of every day of eternity, mostly unnoticed, and that is why I noticed long ago that too much was going unnoticed and began to make a point of noticing. So how could I possibly not notice you? For are you not one of us, a daughter, a sister, a mother, a bride, a mistress, all out there full as you are and at the same time inside all the rest of us, as the law demands, experienced, imagined, longed-for. We are all performers of one sort or another in the theatre of being. There are other theatres of course. There is the theatre of the church, with its rich and colorful sets and relics and robes and red shoes and purple sashes and even incense of myrrh and whatever. There is the theatre of the school with its uniformity of desks and blackboards, books, and paper and pencils. By God, boy, by Heaven, girl, you're going to learn or you're going to die, so learn to learn. Learn German, Latin, mathematics, grammar, piano, trombone, theology, biology, trigonometry, cooking, home economics, and God knows what else. There is the theatre of the street, of the back alleys of the slums of Calcutta, of the sunny steppes of Mongolia, of the inner chambers of the Kremlin, of the outer chambers of the Tokyo Mitsubishi shipyards, of the Fire Department and the Police Department and the Department of Sanitation and the Department of the Unnamed Department. There is the theatre of the absurd whose champion is a

Romanian, Ionesco, the theatre of intellectual games involving identity, whose champion is an Italian, Pirandello, the theatre of despair and meaninglessness whose champion is an Irishman, Beckett, the theatre of loss and regret whose champion is an American, O'Neill, the theatre of gentle amusement about the fraudulence of human nature whose champion is a Frenchman, Moliere, the theatre of abundance, abundance, unbelievable variety in the character of the human being, male and female whose champion is an Englishman, Shakespeare, and there is the theatre of comic tenderness about unidentified sorrow about being human whose champion is a Russian, Chekhov. And so on and so forth—I've left out ten times as much as I've gathered together, of course, but that is how we do, and it's all right. There's only one play, and each of us *lives* it, and knows all of its ways, and this is it, yourself, myself, himself, herself, and for all we know St. Stephens just out there a bit and the cobblestones of the Graben, our beloved Promenade, and the patient soil under every city in the world waiting for God knows what to happen, could it be something incalculably vast in the explosion line perhaps? Bringing down everything and leaving the soil free at last to exhale, having inhaled so many billion years ago nobody can guess how many. What play?

ALICE

I was Mary Pickford in "Jesus Christ Super Son," that's what play.

VAN

Ah, yes, yes, I saw you. Innocence itself. How right, how right.

SCENE 9

This time the interval concerns itself with a very hard but very necessary and very possible approximation in music, by Loris Tjeknavorian, of the crying of newborn infants, a whole panoply of such basic and wondrous sounds by means of violin, cello,

179

trumpet, clarinet, French horn, tuba, trombone, and even piano and timpani, somehow. SCHMIDT *goes out for his usual change of costume and character, and* ALICE *does the same. The* BOY *comes in holding the hand of a small girl in the form of a doll, and he walks about the table where the* ENCEINTE GIRL *sits, but she does not seem to know who or what he is.* HO *comes out of the kitchen to survey the scene, then comes back holding the sleeve of an old coat as if it were a child, and the handlebar of a tricycle, and walks-dances behind the* BOY, *incognito. At the end of the wa-wa concerto, so to call it,* HO *goes back into the kitchen, and the* BOY *back to the Graben, and suddenly there is silence.*

VAN

What's all this silence about?

SCHMIDT

Well, the human race was just born, so the silence is about death, wouldn't you say?

VAN

I would *not*. What death? Remember, I happen to be an Armenian. We don't believe in death. Some of our best boys and girls have very nearly established the total falsity of the whole theory of death. They have done it in terms of science, I mean. Not fantasy, not ambition, not fear, not hope and expectation. So what do you mean the silence is about death? Explain yourself, Hayek, Bahrone?

SCHMIDT

No, Sir, not Alec Aroon, whoever he is, another Armenian, I presume, immortal, I presume, a student perhaps in the first class of the Mekhitarists almost 200 years ago, I presume. Deathless, unkillable, as we have all gladly and sadly noticed— gladly because if you can do it we can do it. Sadly, because you were driven to deathlessness by pogrom and massacre, violence and deportation without food and water, and something, something like death happened to a million of you, and yet all over the world here you are, every one of you still in the play of being, still speaking your own language, still being proud Christians, still printing your daily papers like printing the daily gospel, new chapters of the Holy Bible every day, and your weekly political magazines, and your monthly literary magazines full of the most astonishing poems and stories and essays, and your quarterly magazines of history. Not Alec Aroon, Sir, whoever he is, but just for size, let's say, Friedrich Nietzsche, heart-broken for being madly in love with Richard Wagner's wife, and Richard, Richard, there are so many great Richards, especially The Third, Richard Wagner watching the frustration and torment of his young friend Friedrich Nietzsche about the body of Richard Wagner's wife concealed by exciting garments as she moves about in the drawing room of the lavish home, the daughter of a famous man, whose name (and address) I forget. I am Nietzsche, that fool. Suppose Richard Wagner had conveniently died, perhaps of a fish bone in his throat, and so his wife was now his widow and free to accept the adoration of Friedrich Nietzsche, do you think they would have embraced and celebrated one another in the classic clutch of passion, of fornication if you like, or of fathering and mothering the human race? Do you think it would have happened? Do you think for a minute that Richard Wagner's widow would indeed accept the sweet soft sentimental adoration of Friedrich Nietzsche?

VAN

Yes, I do, and not for only a minute, but for an hour, a day, a year, a lifetime, indeed forever.

SCHMIDT

I am astonished, after what you said about the theatre, this belief of yours about a silly love-sick boy and a hearty well-loved woman surprises me. Are you sure you are an Armenian? They are usually so intelligent, so sophisticated without forfeiting their everlasting innocence, so aware of the truth about the human heart. For centuries their marriages were arranged, and it made magnificent sense, both for them and for the rest of us. Am

I to understand that you actually believe that Friedrich Nietzsche would take to his bosom the widow of Richard Wagner and be successful in this taking of the majestic fort of that body and soul?

VAN

I do.

SCHMIDT

Very well, then, be good enough, Armenian, to tell me why.

VAN

Because I am a believer.

SCHMIDT

Yes, and a waiter in a coffee house.

VAN

Wrong, wrong-o! Sir. A waiter in the world itself, the same as yourself, waiting for, not truth, but knowledge, grace.

SCENE 10

Clown ballet involving HO *and dummies, newspapers, coffee cups and pots.*

ALICE

It says here, A man has got to give his performance. Woe unto the man who has not *rehearsed.*

SCHMIDT

It says *where?*

ALICE

In this coffee cup, of course. Where else? In the daily papers of Vienna? Don't make me laugh. Paris? Rome? Berlin?

London? Moscow? New York? Dear, dear, no, no, a thousand times no, a million times no, they publish only information, I suppose it might be called. Coffee grounds pass along better messages, more like art than statistics you might say, but even coffee grounds turn out to be belittling of half the human race, half the entirety, half the reality, half the potential, no wonder we are taking so long to really begin to be who we are. A man—a man—not a woman, not anybody, not person, a *man* has got to give his performance. Woe unto the man who has not rehearsed.

SCHMIDT

I must say you're much more interesting than most of the men I have ever met, man and boy these many years, and traveling very nearly everywhere. I am astonished—in a way. You look at coffee grounds in a cup and you decide that instead of forming a picture the coffee grounds assume the shape of writing and you come right out and announce that—how does that go again?

ALICE

A man has got to give his performance. Woe unto the man who has not rehearsed.

SCHMIDT

Yes, exactly. But why did you decide that the coffee grounds said those particular words? Performance. Woe. Rehearsed. A man has got to act his part, in other words. And if he doesn't work at it he's going to hear from somebody, in other words. Why didn't the coffee grounds say something else, something more charitable about women, for instance—you are a woman, and if I may say a very excellent specimen.

ALICE

Kindly do not put me in the laboratory. Don't forget I come from a long line of men, as well as women, and many of those men had short tempers, and so do I, deep down, although custom and training, they have not failed to make me feel embarrassed about even feeling like *stopping* anybody from being a fool at my expense. I am a woman, period, but my male ancestors, all of them have been men, just as all of your female ancestors have been women, as somebody said not so long ago.

SCHMIDT

Quite right, quite right, and I apologize, but it is true that we have fallen into the habit of speaking in vast generalities about that very element of our truth which does not lend itself to anything more general than the unaccountable specific. Somebody is somebody. Somebody is not somebody else. We have not got that quite straight after all these years. Jung, also Viennese, may have said something or other about that, but if he did I don't remember what it was. As he became older Alfred, if that *is* his first name, but if it isn't let's pretend it is, Alfred Jung, growing old began to think quite a lot about life after death, as the saying is, and this in turn compelled many comic-minded people to enjoy a jocular turn of thought, belittling Alfred Jung, saying, Who cares about life after death, how about a little life after birth? Now, here of course we have the specific word, life, and it does not have a gender. It is not male, it is not female, it is either both or it is something beyond each. But what I am really saying, really trying to say, is that I like the cleverness of your choice of words out of the coffee grounds, and your performance of the words, demonstrating that you, at any rate, have not neglected to rehearse. Am I right?

ALICE

Wrong. I spoke helplessly, brooding about the predicament.

SCHMIDT

What predicament are you thinking of?

ALICE

The predicament of whales and porpoises, if you must ask your kindergarten questions.

SCHMIDT

They are amply defended by all sorts of people in penitentiaries, and in colleges, and in the streets, and upon highways and railroad tracks. Tell me, please, the predicament you are melancholy about which compelled you to decide that the coffee grounds said if it is necessary or only *desirable* to act, it is a good idea to see to it, and to work at it. Common sense of course, but why didn't the coffee grounds impel you to express other melancholy words, somewhat in the form of a proverb, or a saying?

ALICE

Because I am female, and she is female, and she is pregnant, and that's the predicament. There's no father, but *she* has *got* to be the mother, or commit murder, kill the son.

SCENE 11

VAN *leads all of the others in an improvised song along the lines of,* "Here we are, aren't we? Luckier than anybody else. Luckier than the two or three that did not quite get born. Luckier than the little tiny solar systems far away that did not splinter off the first explosion. Here we are, each of us a tiny solar system so far away there is no measure to say, dislocated and nameless, and gone before its own arrival, tiny tiny but a thousand times larger than our own solar system—sun, moon, and earth. Here we are damned fools sitting in the shade and sipping silly coffee, where will it ever end? Who will win? Where will the loser go? What will the winner do? In the meantime, in the meantime, Lord, Lord, in the mean mean mean meantime, here we are desperate and lonely trying to find out what we are waiting for. We fail, we fail, and order another coffee."

VAN

What fools, what fools, what innocent fools, every one of us. Thank God I've got easy work to do. Ho, ha, but look who's

185

come to visit us. Oh, dear gorgeous girl, flower of folly, thank you for letting us behold you—and please sit down and let me bring you a coffee. Guarden Offizier, will you be good enough to release the elbow of that celestial fragment of insatiable desire and just get back to the Graben, and to Heidelberg, and to Mayerling after the double-suicide and do your usual Teutonic duty to the human race.

OFFIZIER IN OPERETTA COSTUME

This *man* claims somebody here can vouch for him. Otherwise he's going back to the chorus. He is not ready to sing solo.

VAN

We've all gone mad, that's what. The human race went mad a million years ago and nobody noticed. So how can we demand that we make sense? Our science has left out just about everything. Our religion put the emphasis in the wrong place. Our art tried to adore truth but succeeded only in pretending to adore beauty. Cheeee!

HO

What's going on?

VAN

Oh, get back to the kitchen and stick to your good work. Ho, Ho, Hovakim, you are a coffee-maker. Offizier, you said *man,* but where is the man? You continue to hold the elbow of a gorgeous woman. Why? If she has broken a city ordinance of some kind, take her to jail, or take her home so your wife can see what a real woman looks like, or take her to the Park across from the Hilton Hotel and walk with her along the banks of the sunken river and talk love to her the way so many Viennese boys and girls do. Why bring her into the Haydakor Coffee House, we are new in the game, we have not yet built up a fame based upon the kind of people who like to come here to sit and sip and think and dream and chat and fall silent. Madame, please accept my thanks for permitting me to behold your magnificent voluption—I always forget I am a voluptuary until I see such voluption and then I am so mortified by the terrible loss over the years that I instantly lose all of my physical appeal for a member of the opposite sex and act and talk like a stupid, stunned, sick school boy ready for rapery, rampage, the taking of the Sabine women, but denied mercilessly, denied the rampage and riot of such simple ritual truth. Madame, I have a small room in the back, with a cot, and certainly a floor, and these things—the cot has a red and white checkered woven cover and the floor has good firm oak planks which I believe you might enjoy, in a manner of speaking. Oh, Christ Almighty, just as I said, just as I said. Please sit down, do not be intimidated by the Guarden Offizier, whatever may have been the wrong which entitled him to seize you by the elbow, by God, what could it be, and I have a little money by means of which to satisfy his lust for profit in all things. How much do you want?

OFFIZIER

You must be out of your head. You've got to be mad. I didn't interrupt because I was fascinated. Are you just released from bedlam, from the lunatic asylum, the looney bin, or what?

SCHMIDT

Or, what, perhaps. I'll vouch for the man, Offizier. I believe I know him. Life is too long for enormous errors, the little ones will do. He solicited you, is that correct, Offizier? Alfie solicited you, Offizier?

GIRL

Alfie? Alfie? I didn't mention his name, did I? I certainly didn't intend to. Is that you, Alfie? Oh, Alfie, I've never seen you that way before. You make me look like a drudge. You make all women look ugly.

ALICE

Maybe so, but he can't get pregnant.

OFFIZIER

Am I to understand then, Miss, that you do indeed vouch for him?

GIRL

Oh, yes, yes, he's my husband. Well, he is the father of my son, to be.

ALICE

But he has a husband of his own somewhere in the woodwork.

OFFIZIER

(Heels click—Salute) Vienna will let it go, this time, Madame, Sir, but watch it.

SCENE 12

The interval is devoted to hush and thought and melancholy, as it were, while everybody sits and thinks and scarcely remembers to sip coffee. And then suddenly a loud piece of jazz is heard coming from the Graben, and VAN *goes to the door to look at the players. The music is banjo, clarinet, drum, and voice: about appetite, hunger, food and drink.*

VAN

Americans. I *think.* Maybe not, though. We have our own Americans these days, too. Blue jeans, cowboy boots, cowboy hats, cowboy blue cotton shirts, cowboy belts, cowboy brains, cowboy manners. All fraudulent. Well, you certainly had me fooled, Alfie boy. You're still gorgeous, but I don't believe I would ever knowingly make love to somebody with the same sexual organs that I have.

SCHMIDT

Why not?

SCENE 12

VAN

If I didn't know, if I believed my eyes, in such a relationship, in an animal relationship, so to put it, many a man and also many a woman has surely fooled the other man, and even the husband. I mean, I knew a very sincere father who told me he was absolutely befuddled when he deduced by means of logic that for a rather long time his devoted wife, the mother of their four children, was directing him to the back entrance. He never told her he had made the discovery but she found out for herself because he never used that entrance again. So with all of the variations of animals together it would be very easy for a gorgeous piece of tail like Alfie to make a man believe he was putting the blocks to a woman. I certainly was ready only a little while ago. Alfie, oh, Alfie, why aren't you a woman? Don't tell me, I know, I know, you are, you *are* a woman, and more, you are more than a woman, but I'm asking why aren't you a woman with a woman's parts, by birth, not by Danish surgery, because we all know that such surgery and hormones can work many miracles.

ALICE

Except one. She can't get pregnant. So Alfie here has got this dear *girl* pregnant, so he can go home to his husband holding their darling first-born infant.

GIRL

First-born? I wouldn't do it for him *twice*. I'm not sure I want to do it for him once even. Would we then, Alfie, be man and wife, like ordinary dull stupid unimaginative people? That's all I ask. With all my fragility and fear I'll have our darling child, my own personal gift to God and the glory of His great heart and mind, and you can give the child to your—your—husband? And then shut the door in his face and come home with me to our true love and life, is that right, Alfie? Alfie? Why don't you answer me? Are you thinking about the joy of our true life together, as I am? Is that the reason you can't, you won't speak, won't answer me? Or are you answering me and I am not tuned in—because I happen to be *enceinte* and terrified? Give you my child, my own flesh and blood with head and eyes and nostrils and perfect toes and fingers and his own private privates, what am I saying? Alfie, I can't give you my boy, my man, it goes against nature, it goes against everything. Let your stupid runty grunty husband *adopt* a child if he has got to have a child. They are letting that happen nowadays, you know. Everybody is so understanding it's sickening. For God's sake, Alfie, I'm pregnant, by *you*—do you want to take away my life and give it to some silly interior decorator?

ALFIE

He's a cop. The gays broke down that barrier, too. I'm the hair dresser. I did your hair, didn't I?

ALICE

If he's a cop what were you doing out there soliciting *another* cop? Are you queer for cops, is that it?

ALFIE

How vulgar. We don't use words like queer, fairy, fag. There is just as much justification for the usage of refinement of language among us as among you. Vulgarity is just as vulgar with us as with you. We frown on it. We like nicety. We like delicacy. We *worship* witty refinement.

ALICE

The predicament I was thinking about, then, Sir.

SCHMIDT

Yes, so I see, and how is it to be resolved, is that the question?

ALICE

Really? You are inviting me to rehearse, are you? Speaking for the little pregnant child and for the life that has started in her belly? To be or not to be? Is that what you are inviting me to rehearse? Shall the procedure continue or shall it be stopped?

Shall the billion billion fragments that are to form brain, bone, skin, blood, vein, cell, and all, be permitted to move forward in unaccountable mystery until the human race has another son? If so, if you are inviting me to rehearse, let's say very well, I have done so.

SCHMIDT

But what is to be, and what is not to be? Shall you have your gift to God?

GIRL

I don't know. I want to die.

SCENE 13

The interval concerns itself with a Salvation Army style band making music on the Graben, and an almost-heard exhortation of a Captain of the Army urging the Promenading People to stop and think a little about eternity: "I say unto you unless a man gets ready for eternity he is going to miss the bus as sure as there is a heaven and a hell. And I say unto you do not be forever prisoners of food and drink, meat and wine, Sacher chocolate and Demel dainties, for you will wind up in the hospital with a bad case of a mysterious new disease that is very simple but incognito, and if you want to know the name of that deadly disease my friends, ladies and gentlemen of Vienna and Liverpool, boys and girls of Boston and Geneva, well, the name is nothing new at all, it is death. So I say unto you do not turn away and laugh up your sleeves at me, an old fool who used to be one of you, but is now saved. Come along, come along with me and also be saved, for it is the saving of the soul that is really the one thing." *Boom, boom, tambourine, flute, and the compact horn that looks like a fine achievement of displaced plumbing.*

VAN

I love them—that worry about me, beginning with themselves, they keep the faith while I keep the books, good God, it just won't do, will it?

HO

How many coffees?

VAN

No coffees, I'm just keeping the books. Well, then, bring me one, please, and let me sit here like a customer and just sip and think.

HO

Ready and waiting, one for you, and one for me, and I'll sit with you.

ALICE

It is good for the servants now and then to become royalty. I have always believed in that. Indeed I have never quite been able to believe at all in royalty, even though I have sensed in my own self the old delusions of kings and, pardon me young man, queens, among my ancestors, ranting and raving, because the same things that have harassed everybody else are harassing them, too: disrespect mainly. You sit well, the two of you, with your noses, and your ancient memories, and God knows what secrets you sit with, as we are always wondering about so many of us—gypsies, for instance, it is all secrets with the gypsies. And Jews, secrets all the way, even when they are famous comedians in the big cities all over the world they are keeping secrets, and no goy, I *believe* that's the word for outsiders, can come within a mile of the secrets: the secret of the secrets. And after the gypsies and the Jews, farmers, they keep to themselves their experiences involving seeds and tides, light and the phases of the moon, leafery and bud, blossom and bee, and all we see is but what the farmers bring forth out of secrecy. And eat it. Bankers, also. Garbage-collectors. Lawyers. Accountants.

Floor-walkers. Doctors. Secrets. Secrets. They live and die keeping their secrets, and as you sit and sip that coffee I am sure you are keeping Armenian secrets. Don't do that, please, all of you, gypsies, Jews, farmers, bankers, garbage-collectors, lawyers, accountants, floor-walkers, doctors, and Armenians, tell us all your secrets. Tell us, please, before it is too late.

VAN

I can't speak for that motley conglomerate, but I can say for the Armenians, or at any rate for *this* Armenian, myself, you are not really mistaken, most likely, but you must include yourself in the group, for there are census-takers and they ask a lot of questions. They are in touch with the tax collector. They turn in reports to the government. How many bathrooms in your corner of the empty warehouse where you go every night to get ready for tomorrow, God willing. That's the kind of secret they want you to tell them. And you do, you do, because if you don't they will report that you keep secrets and are probably an assassin with a compulsion to do in the royal family, as you were saying. No bathrooms in my corner of the warehouse, you say. I manage here and there the way my ancestors did. Yes, I do have secrets, and yes, I do keep them, but it isn't because I am unwilling to pass them along, it is because nobody, nobody, by God, is interested in them, and so it must be with the gypsies and the Jews and all of the Armenians and all of the others. And I don't pass along my secrets because if the truth is told I really don't know them that well myself. I know they're there, from so many of my people, each of them an enormity but totally unknown to me by name or nature. I can't for the life of me make heads or tails of them, eye or ear, hand or foot, nose or mouth. When I shut up, fall silent, just sit, look at my face and you will see the same keeping of secrets that you see when you look at the face of a sprawling lion either in a cage at the zoo or in a jungle. Or a horse, or a dog, or a cow, or a bear, any creature with eyes keeps secrets. Nobody can say what he has seen.

SCENE 14

The interval is walking as if it were dance, art itself.

ALFIE

Why are we here? I mean, why are we *here?* I mean, there
are reasons we are here, so why? I mean, why did we *come* here?

GIRL

Oh, Alfie, we came here for luck, don't you remember? You
said somebody you know told you that going to the Haydakor
Coffee House brings a person good luck, so in our longing for
a solution to our predicament we came here to see if it is true,
if there is such a place, and there is, and we are here. We came
here to see if there is any truth to your friend's belief that this
place brings a person good luck.

ALFIE

Not you. I was asking *them?* Why are we here, Sir?

SCHMIDT

In the Haydakor Coffee House, or do you mean in Vienna, or
in Europe rather than in America, for instance, or do you mean
in the world itself, on earth, that is, among the lot of us and
our brothers and sisters the animals at home and in the zoos?

ALFIE

All that and more. I mean, why are we each of us in this body,
how did it happen that everything conspired so flawlessly in
time and place and action to put me here, and you there, and
here and there everybody each in this body—think of the
leftovers who were not so consigned, and are without body,
each of them, by the uncountable billions of billions, each of
them unable to ask, Why me? Who was it that said it can be
an accident, because sometimes I'm sure he's mistaken and then
sometimes I know, I absolutely know, I shiver with the

excitement of the knowing that he's right, it can't, it just can't can't can't be an accident.

SCHMIDT

Steady, old man. Easy, now. Well, then. Are you all right?

ALFIE

Yes, quite, thank you, and you can't answer the question, nobody can, so let's just forget it, shall we, and talk the way we always talk—gossip, gossip, gossip. Did Napoleon have a big one?

ALICE

Tiny, tiny, as a matter of fact. Many a mighty man who ought to have a big one actually has a tiny nose.

ALFIE

I don't want any more gossip. I can't stand it, really. I am pins and needles. Why are we here?

SCHMIDT

Very well, then, you asked for it. We are here to witness the birth.

ALFIE

Of my son? To give to my husband?

GIRL

Good God Almighty, will you please get a load of him? The most gorgeous woman from the streets of Vienna and you heard him, you heard him. So what am I doing here? Who am I supposed to be? And when I give birth to my son as my own personal adoring gift to God, who is my son supposed to be, my own, God's own, or this gorgeous woman's counterfeit kidnapped fraudulent whimsical piece of some kind of prolonged silly pleasure to some kind of weird policeman? That man there who could be anybody's father says, We are here to witness the birth. And the gorgeous woman asks, he has the hideous effrontery to ask, Of my son? To give to my husband. Oh, Alfie, Alfie, how could you, and you are so good at doing hair. You did mine so beautifully, and then the lower hair, to have it look like the moustache of Frederick The Great, which excited you so—oh, you know, or I wouldn't be pregnant right now. I never saw you so—masculine. So here you are now so feminine you are able to believe that my pregnancy is your pregnancy, my son is your son, my gift to God is your gift to your husband, and so where is my husband to accept my gift? That gorgeous woman, Alfie. Why? Talk about secrets. What's your secret?

ALFIE

I have no secret. I left the closet almost instantly. But if you don't mind there are things I must talk about man to man with this man.

GIRL

Oh, Alfie, Alfie, what a fool you are, and what a bigger fool I am to love you just the same, or also to love you, or to love part of you, God help me, you do entertain a girl, you know, with your superior femininity. Nobody can pass along the dirt about everybody else the way you can, Alfie.

ALFIE

I wish to speak to this gentleman, please. Another time I will speak to you. Hold your water. Keep your pants on. Just try to hold your water, please. Is that asking too much? The birth of my son, Sir? Is that the birth we are here to witness, Sir?

SCHMIDT

In a way, yes, but if the truth is told I was thinking of another birth, as a matter of fact. Thinking of myself as one of the three wise men, as it were, and the totally unastonished gentlemen at that table, Ho the coffee-maker and Van the Coffee House waiter, the other two. Melchior and so on and so forth, what are their names, I always loved the story, never understood it. The birth in other words of the human race.

ALICE

Half the human race, if you don't mind.

SCHMIDT

Yes, yes, quite right. Half, then.

SCENE 15

Opera. Aria, "Did Jesus cry when he came forth, the way I cried when I was born? Or did the son of God look around at the faces of cows and sheep and men and women and burst into laughter? Was it simple joy, or was it terrible agony? They tell us as soon as we can understand. They tell us we cried and came alive. We joined the hopeless mob of victims victimizing victims and themselves. We wept and started out. We crawled and stood and walked and used the mouth for the taking of food and drink and the making of sounds outside of language and then inside: Mama. Dada. Mama. Dada. Oh, boy, oh, joy, where do we go from here?''

ALFIE

The birth of the human race. Well, it is a pleasant conceit, at that. But thanks, I'd rather not. Thanks loads, I'd like my son to be just a wee bit less than all that, just a nice gurgling little gift will be enough for me, and him, and him, the infant and the father, my husband.

GIRL

I'm getting sick.

ALICE

Yes, it is sickening, little girl. We've had the birth, in any case. Isn't this, then, the opposite of that, sir?

197

SCHMIDT

No, I don't think so, I have this feeling that the opposite is also birth, is a confirmation of birth, and is otherwise a kind of event both beyond memory and experience. Nobody has ever told any man how he died, but every man is told how he was born.

ALFIE

I didn't major in philosophy at U.C.L.A.

SCHMIDT

You're an American, then? U.C.L.A.? The University of California at Los Angeles? You don't look like an American.

ALFIE

I am a Teuton, out of Offenbach, Strauss, Freud, and all of the other famous Viennese, but I am also an American, and who isn't? Any more? These days? They have gone to work and surpassed us all in the superiority of their deterioration, they show us all the shortest route to total freedom, license, experimentation, individuality, irresponsibility, pleasure, pleasure, and then the supreme pleasure of steady self-destruction with red lights and purple shadows and satisfaction straight ahead and steadfast endurance of an unendurable and all for itself and for death. Oh, excuse me, please, I didn't mean to use that crude word. Orgasm, then, rather than that crude word. Death. I look like an American all right. At U.C.L.A. I majored in theatrical arts with emphasis on scenery, costumes, and make-up. My experience has been that offal itself if properly costumed and made-up can seem as radiant as buttercup, sunflower, and rose. That's what theatre is and what it is for. To tell us nice lies. Your lies, Sir, are also meant to be nice, but are they really? How can we find it nice that in the birth of one infant the entire lot of us is born.

SCHMIDT

Or the other way around perhaps, wouldn't you say? In the birth of all of us each of us is himself, how did you put it, please, dear woman—I thought you put it very neatly.

ALICE

How did I put *what,* sir?

SCHMIDT

Where you were Mary Pickford. Or Mary Magdalen. Or Mary Stuart Queen of Scots? Or Mary Miles Minter?

ALFIE

Or Mary McGinnis, my own dear mother, please let me cry about her.

GIRL

I *say* I'm getting sick. Don't you understand?

ALICE

What is it, girl? Sir, do you mean, then, Mary Pickford in "Jesus Christ Super Son?" And the other way around is that when anybody is born it is the birth of Super Son and Super Daughter, and all of us. Girl, what is it? Is it gas? We saw you dance. There's no pregnancy showing.

GIRL

I can't hold the water. I can't. I try and try, but I can't. Oh.

ALFIE

Oh? You're not losing my son, are you, you silly girl. Can't you even do what you are born to do, made to do, designed to do, you terribly inferior thing you. Must you lose my son, must you piss away my soul, must you spoil my fun, murder my expectations of more and more pleasure, with pleasure kill me, you foolish fraudulent female? *(Alfie dies)*

VAN

Come with me, come with me, I'll make you comfortable.

SCHMIDT

Well, does anybody know anything about mouth to mouth first aid for this outraged man?

ALICE

It wouldn't help. The gorgeous man has had the last fun in the tradition he pursued and longed-for. He died unhappy only by word of mouth. He died happier than almost anybody who has ever died, although he probably didn't know it, and now it's too late. Why are we here?

SCHMIDT

Well, we can always answer a question by asking another. Why shouldn't we be here? If there's a better place to be, where is it, pray tell? Where do you get this kind of gypsy, Jewish, Armenian telling of secrets, a little something like the truth?

SCENE 16

THE LARK *chants, with special music approximately crying-and-laughing.*

SCHMIDT

Well, we were expecting a birth and we got a death. Do you believe in death? Was she pregnant or was it gas? The three Wise Men followed the Star of Bedlam not Bethlehem or the Star of Babylon, of the Babble of Tongues, that is, the Star of Fable, of Fantasy, of Folly, riding their little animals, their asses, their donkeys, their Biblical and Ancient servants of Man with their sad eyes, and they came to the Coffee House called Haydakor—and somebody hollered something like, For unto you a Savior is born, or some such joyous absurdity, and the Three of Them believed it, because by nature they were believers. But did their little animals believe it with their patient eyes and their small bodies bearing heavy burdens? And even after the Boy told us all, All ye who are heavy-laden, put your burden upon me, even after he said that, the donkeys of the three boys either didn't hear, or heard and didn't understand, or didn't believe, and *kept* their burdens, the three wise men— Mesach, Shadrach, and Nabednego, poor bastards.

ALICE

Those are not the names of the three wise men. They are the names of three other bastards.

SCHMIDT

Well, you can't expect a great man also to be correct in every little detail of legend and lore. There were three of them, and legend is stronger in arithmetic than in anything else. Three is three, but all the rest of it is open to dispute.

ALICE

A great man? Is that what you said? Do you, then, think of yourself as such? A great man, exempt from the usage of the right names of the heroes of the fables. How shall we know you are a great man, then?

SCHMIDT

You shall not know, of course, for you do not *need* to know. I know, and that is the end of it. And the other two, they also are great men, come to witness the birth at last of the human race itself, in one person, a male child, not even twins, a male child and a female child, instead the human race ran down the mother's leg like spoiled water, and a male child from about thirty years ago went berserk in the soul and dropped dead. Is there a meaning here, allegorical or actual? Or are we here, after all, to sip coffee and to pass the time of day until it is night, and then to pass the time of night? I mean, he died. He was certainly taken away by the appropriate people. What were his last words, again? Everybody is interested in the last words of everybody? What did he say?

ALICE

He was raving. He was sick. He may have had a heart condition all his life. It may have been part of a good many conditions that permitted him to believe in himself as he did and to disbelieve in his father as he did. He ranted and he raved and he died. He was shouting and screaming apparently at the poor pregnant girl for not holding her water, although we can also suspect that he was actually ranting and raving at his father and mother, and the human race itself, flawless but also flawed, *flawed* in all of its physical embodiment of its non-physical essence, its spirit, its memory, its fear, and joy, and sorrow. He was more probably ranting and raving at everybody and at everything for no better reason than the reason that he was what he was, he was who he was, and it came to him suddenly that in a moment he was not going to be even *that*—and it drove him fruity, as the saying goes, and he died, he died.

SCHMIDT

Do you believe in death?

ALICE

I don't disbelieve in it any more than I disbelieve in birth. Although I do suspect that the best people do not make it. The real human race has never peopled the earth and made the human world, which as we know is totally without foundation and totally fraudulent, but also the only place we have.

SCHMIDT

You say the best people do not get born? Very strange, I must say.

ALICE

Even so, strange or not strange, the best people do not get born because their progenitors, their fathers and their mothers, are too refined to be equal to the crudity of procreation.

SCHMIDT

Amazing. I'm amazed. To look at you, nobody would suspect that you know such things, can say such things, nobody would suspect that you have studied at the greatest universities of the world.

ALICE

I suppose I have, at that, although not the way you mean. I have never been to any kind of school at all after the age of eleven when I became a woman. But I have been married six times, and have a child from each marriage, which of course was the reason in each instance why I *got* married...that is to provide a father for the child, each of them amazing, as you say.

SCENE 17

Whale music, fish music, ocean music, echo music, faraway music.

HO

Coffee, then. Compliments of the Haydakor management, so to say.

ALICE

Thank you, and how is she? I mean, I did everything I could for her, and the doctor came and went, and said she must rest, so is she resting?

HO

Yes, she's all right, she's fast asleep, the pill will keep her asleep for another short time. And Van is sitting there looking at her.

SCHMIDT

Why? Has *he* gone mad, too?

HO

Van? Don't be silly. The doctor said she might want to do away with herself when she discovers the loss. He said somebody should be ready to speak to her—and it had better be a man, a Father, rather than a woman, a Mother. So Van has accepted the part in the play.

ALICE

I'm ready to be of help. Sometimes a doctor can be mistaken, even in Vienna. If she wants the solace of a Mother, I've had quite a lot of experience. Three boys, three girls, six Fathers, one Mother, six races, and each of them an astonishment, especially in the beginning. And then steadily, steadily, don't ask me why, they lost it, they became totally human, they became adults, three pimps, and three whores.

SCHMIDT

How can you say that about your own kids?

ALICE

The boys are in business, and they are considered honorable, but they are pimps. The three girls are married to rather rich and even famous men whom they delight in bed and also provide with children, but they are whores. Should we call the boys solid citizens and the girls good wives and mothers? I would rather call them what they are and to love them just the same, or even more. Only hypocrites and weaklings give pimps and whores a bad name. They use them when nobody is looking or when they themselves aren't looking and then they are filled with guilt and cry out for God and Mama and Papa to please please forgive them—and it never occurs to them that Papa was a pimp and Mama was a whore, and that's before the little complications of reversal of roles when Papa became Mama, and Mama Papa, and the boy became a girl and the girl became a boy.

SCHMIDT

Amazing. Amazing. I believe it, but I don't believe a word of it, not a word. But of course I can't say why. Why don't I believe it?

HO

Because you don't want to. Because if you believe it you are also one of them, take your choice, pimp or whore.

SCHMIDT

Humbug, nonsense, stuff and feathers, talk, and talk is cheap.

HO

Well, enjoy the coffee, enjoy the chair, each of you enjoy a small table—we used to have a man write poems at a table. He wrote real honest-to-God poems, because he showed us a whole book of them.

SCHMIDT

What happened to him? If that's the point.

HO

He just stopped coming here. You'll stop coming here, too, each of you. There are other Coffee Houses, other places, and why you came here in the first place has got to be something nobody can really know, and you will finally stop coming here in the same way. But of course it is the opinion of Van and myself, and indeed our experience that others will come here, and we shall serve them good coffee and become slightly acquainted with them and trade words and courtesies for as long as they like, and so it goes, so it goes. We are in business, pimps if you like, but for a good cause, and so it's all right, we believe, it's all right.

SCHMIDT

A good cause? What is your good cause? To restore Armenia to its lands and glory?

HO

Well, thank you, that's very thoughtful of you, and it is true that there is scarcely an Armenian or a half-Armenian or a quarter-Armenian, even, who does not believe that if there is a God in heaven and anything like justice in the affairs of men that Armenia will one day be truly Armenia again. But that is not the good cause I am thinking of, which is simply to earn money to send to needy members of the family in other places of the world, and to bring to Vienna a few of our nearest of kin to put into the famous Mekhitarian school to learn to read and write both classic and modern Armenian.

SCHMIDT

Why? Why is that so important?

HO

Because there is much good writing to read in the Armenian language.

SCHMIDT

Amazing. I have no such feeling about my nearest of kin, or my own son, and my own daughter—I was married to the same woman for ten years and I was delighted by my kids, again especially while they were under eleven years of age. They don't read the great German writers. They don't read anything. What did I do wrong?

SCENE 18

Children's games music: rope-jump, hop-scotch, racing-a-rosey, and all.

ALICE

Well, we've seen it all now, haven't we, just sitting in a cool pleasant place with nothing more to do than notice one another in passing and to remember our people of long ago, especially of childhood, and our near and dear, especially in the immediate family, so now what, now what? One day, as he said, we shall not come back, we know that. *Why do we keep coming back these days, then? And especially why don't we get up and leave right now?*

SCHMIDT

I don't know about you, but I have got some more thinking to do. And I want to find out how it is going to end. I have this compulsive curiosity about ourselves, I guess you might say. *Was* she pregnant?

ALICE

Oh, yes. She was.

SCHMIDT

Was she pregnant with the human race, I mean with *all* of us.

ALICE

Yes, I think so. All of us is not a great deal as you know, it is mainly repetition, and apparently meaningless repetition at that. Why do they hate you? Have you decided? Does your decision make sense?

SCHMIDT

Who? My kids? Well, the son has *got* to. Nature, you know. But the daughter—that's something else again. Such a *play* of

207

love, in letters, in telegrams, in telephone calls, all the while
staying far away. Didn't any of your kids, your boys, hate you?

ALICE

They all hated me. A mother is a hateful person. But I just
couldn't be bothered about it. I have always been myself, and
that's as far as the trolley goes, isn't it? I mean if you are yourself
and you accept yourself then it is all right for whoever will,
or must, to hate you. Or for that matter to love you. I don't
favor the hate, but I'm not all that keen about the love either.
I rather like a little comedy, a little intelligence, a little casualness
about it all. It makes the going easier. Well, I see that the dear
dummies who sat at the two tables are gone, our beloved
unknown friends are gone from the Haydakor Coffee House
on Graben not far from St. Stephens. Not a word from them,
not a peep. Who are they with their sweet faces and their awful
silence? Ourselves? Well, I feel their departure is a vague loss.
I feel a little lonely, a little *lonelier*. For myself, of course. For
what's left of me, that is. My own little dummies sitting around
with me all my life have also one by one taken leave of me,
dear mute silly ragdoll girls and mechanical tin marching boys.
What next, then?

VAN

Are you sure? Are you sure you want to walk alone?

GIRL

Yes, quite sure. I'm just fine, thank you. I'm just fine. Was
it?—did the Doctor?—was he able to say? Was it a boy?

VAN

Yes, it was, you can ask her, or him.

ALICE

Yes, it was a fine boy, so try again, there's plenty more where
that came from. I'll hold your arm.

GIRL

No, no, no. Please. I'm just fine, I want to be alone, to mourn
my beloved son, my gift to my Father in Heaven. I'll just walk
across the square to St. Stephens, and light a candle, and then
go home and make a pot of tea and look at the snapshots in
the family album. Goodbye.

ALL

Goodbye, girl. Toodle-oo. Bye bye. Ta ta. Pleasant dreams.
Until tomorrow. Carry on. Hang in. Hold tight. It was fun
knowing you. *Ciao. Arrivederci. Auf Wiedersehen. A bientôt.
Ertak barov.* So long, old pal, old gal. *Adios, Muchachos.*

SCHMIDT

Good heavens, it's after midnight. Well, this is where I came
in. Take care, take care, one and all. *(He mumbles but he is
heard)* Perhaps I should have sent *my* kids to the Mekhitarists.
(Stops, turns) Who? Who was *that* you asked about? Alec
Aroon? Who's he?

VAN

Ah, well, one question sounds like another. My question was,
Hayek, Bahrone?

SCHMIDT

Who's *he,* then?

VAN

Well, my father, my grandfather, my greatgrandfather, and my
mother and her mother and her mother, and my brothers and
sisters and all of us, but especially myself. Hayek, Bahrone is
the question we ask of all strangers. Are you Armenian, Sir?

SCHMIDT

Well, I don't know. I'm not sure. I suppose not, but thanks
for asking... Take care, take care gypsies, Jews, Armenians,

Austrians, Viennese, men, women, boys, and girls. Take care, because if you don't, who will?

HO

Well, that's it, Van. We've had a fair day, a fair day. The place is nice and quiet now. I'll just wipe all the table tops, for tomorrow. The kitchen is in order, so let's let ourselves out and lock the door. We can just make it to the airport in time for the arrival of your sister's son from Beirut to go to the Mekhitarist's school.

VAN

Yes, we'll meet little Dikran, named after the great king, the founder of the walled city of Dikranagert. Nine years old and I've never seen him. We'll put him in school. We'll go there and see him on special occasions and whenever he has permission to do so he will come here to see us and sit at a table and sip a cup of coffee. And what about your brother's daughter, Ho, Ho, Hovakim?

HO

I need to save a little more money, but she will also come by airplane soon. We will all be here together in beautiful Vienna, let me look at the empty tables again, and now we go.

Loud metallic sound of heavy key in heavy lock turning heavy bolt, then again. Then THE LARK *is heard, as if in memory, singing. The lights stay on, the curtain stays up, music joins the singing of the Lark, then very slowly the lights go out, and when all is pitch black something like a dazzling sky full of childhood's galaxies of stars seems to be where the scene had been—the Milky Way, the Big Dipper, the Little Dipper, and so on and so forth. And then there is nothing more, and the play ends.*

SELECTED BIBLIOGRAPHY

Included below are full references to all works cited in the Preface and Introduction. Titles of Saroyan's unpublished works are placed between quotation marks; the same usage is followed in the text of this book.

Lee, Lawrence and Gifford, Barry, *Saroyan, A Biography.* New York: Harper & Row, 1984.

Saroyan, Aram, *William Saroyan.* New York: Harcourt, Brace and Jovanovich, 1983.

Saroyan, William, "Adios Muchachos," 1980 (?), whereabouts of manuscript unknown.

Saroyan, William, *Armenians,* see *William Saroyan: An Armenian Trilogy.*

Saroyan, William, *Births.* Berkeley: Creative Arts Book Company, 1983.

Saroyan, William, *Bitlis,* see *William Saroyan: An Armenian Trilogy.*

Saroyan, William, *Don't Go Away Mad and Two Other Plays.* New York: Harcourt, Brace and Company, 1949.

Saroyan, William, *Haratch,* see *William Saroyan: An Armenian Trilogy.*

Saroyan, William, *Here Comes There Goes You Know Who.* New York: Simon and Schuster, 1961.

Saroyan, William, "How to Write a Great Play," *TV Guide,* March 6, 1976, pp.2-5.

Saroyan, William, *Jim Dandy, Fat Man in a Famine*. New York: Harcourt Brace and Company, 1947.

Saroyan, William, "More Obituaries," manuscript of 1980, William Saroyan Foundation collection, Bancroft Library, University of California, Berkeley.

Saroyan, William, *Not Dying*. New York: Harcourt, Brace & World, 1963.

Saroyan, William, *Obituaries*. Berkeley: Creative Arts Book Company, 1979.

Saroyan, William, "Play Things," manuscript, William Saroyan Foundation collection, Bancroft Library, University of California, Berkeley.

Saroyan, William, *Sam, The Highest Jumper of Them All*. London: Faber and Faber, 1961.

Saroyan, William, *Subway Circus,* in *Razzle-Dazzle*. New York: Harcourt, Brace and Company, 1942; written in 1935.

Saroyan, William, *The Cave Dwellers*. New York: G.P. Putnam's Sons, 1958.

Saroyan, William, "The Daring Young Man on the Flying Trapeze," in *The Daring Young Man on the Flying Trapeze*. New York: Random House, 1934.

Saroyan, William, *The Dogs, or The Paris Comedy and Two Other Plays: Chris Sick, or Happy New Year Anyway, Making Money, and 19 Other Very Short Plays*. New York: Phaedra, 1969.

Saroyan, William, *The Oyster and the Pearl, Perspectives USA,* No. 4 (1953), pp.86-104.

SELECTED BIBLIOGRAPHY

Saroyan, William, *The Time of Your Life*. New York: Harcourt, Brace and Company, 1939.

Saroyan, William, *William Saroyan: An Armenian Trilogy,* edited with an Introductory Essay and Glossary by Dickran Kouymjian. Fresno: The Press at California State University, 1986; includes the plays *Armenian, Bitlis,* and *Haratch.*